AUTUMN & WINTER COLOUR
IN THE GARDEN

AUTUMN & WINTER COLOUR
IN THE GARDEN

Graham Clarke

Ward Lock Limited · London

For Denise

© Ward Lock Ltd 1986

First published in Great Britain in 1986
by Wardlock Limited, 8 Clifford Street,
London W1X 1RB, an Egmont Company

House editor Denis Ingram
Text filmset in Linotype Aster
by Text Filmsetters Ltd, London SE1

Printed and bound in Italy by Canale

British Library Cataloguing in Publication Data

Clarke, Graham
    Autumn & winter colour in the garden.
    1. Gardening
    I. Title
    635   SB453

    ISBN 0-7063-6482-1

ACKNOWLEDGEMENTS

The publishers are grateful to the following for
granting permission for reproduction of colour
photographs: *Amateur Gardening* magazine (pp.7,
21, 22, 28, 53, 56, 67, 79, 81, 87, 93, 101, 105 and
119) and Bob Challinor (p.63). All the remaining
photographs were taken by Bob Challinor.

The publishers are especially grateful to the following persons for allowing their gardens to be
used for photographic purposes: Arthur Billitt of
Clack's Farm (pp.13, 17, 31, 59, 76, 99 and 112);
John Treasure (pp.19, 27, 45, 49, and 85); Felix
and Norma Adams (p.39); and David Thompson
(p.107).

All the line drawings are by Nils Solberg.

CONTENTS

Acknowledgements 4
Preface 6

PART 1 AUTUMN 7

1 Autumn colour 8
2 Trees in autumn 11
3 Shrubs and climbers in autumn 30
4 Border plants in autumn 47
5 Bulbs in autumn 55

PART 2 WINTER 61

6 Winter colour 62
7 Trees in winter 65
8 Shrubs and climbers in winter 71
9 Border plants in winter 84
10 Bulbs in winter 91

PART 3 PLANTING & GENERAL
AFTERCARE 97

11 The art of planting 98
12 General aftercare 110
Appendix: list of useful addresses 124
Index 125

PREFACE

Ask a gardening newcomer to place the seasons in order of importance and they would more than likely put summer first, for its warmth and richness of colour. This would be followed by spring, for its own cool beauty, promising the warmer days ahead. Autumn would probably come third, with its pretty red and gold leaf tints, and bringing up the rear would be winter. To the uninitiated there isn't much to be said for winter: it's cold, bleak, wet and colourless. Or is it?

Ask a keen gardener the same questions, and it is quite likely that the seasons will be quoted in the same order. There may be a change of emphasis, however. Summer and spring are certainly the warmest and most encouraging seasons, but autumn has more beauty than most people realize. Leaf colours are available in every hue; berries of all shapes, sizes and colours hang from trees and shrubs; and a few late-flowering border plants give us the feeling of a prolonged summer.

As for winter, I may regard it as the dullest season, but is that any excuse not to try and make the best of it? With a little searching, your winter garden could be a riot of colour – red, yellow or orange berries, yellow jasmine flowers, blue irises, white and pink viburnum, evergreen and variegated leaves, and the list goes on and on. More so in winter than at any other time, fragrance and scent stand out in the garden. A still morning will capture the hanging fragrance of *Chimonanthus praecox* (winter sweet) or *Viburnum farreri*. We all enjoy dipping our noses into a sweet-smelling flower, and we are just as able to do so during our coldest months as we are in summer.

The aim of this book, therefore, is to explain to you, and show you with our many excellent colour pictures, what delights we can have, if we try, in the otherwise least popular two seasons. I am certainly not suggesting that autumn and winter are more attractive, or in any way better than spring and summer, just that they have many largely undiscovered, or unnoticed colourful attractions.

I hope this book will open your eyes to many new plants, and that you will not consider it a mere textbook, but also an investigation into the often subtle, often dramatic delights of autumn and winter.

G.N.C.

PART 1
AUTUMN

CHAPTER ONE

AUTUMN COLOUR

Autumn, immortalized by Keats as the 'season of mists and mellow fruitfulness', is equally as colourful as spring; indeed, if you are considering 'bulk' of colour, then autumn has the edge. Reds, golds, yellows, browns and russets are the order of the day, and quite beautiful they are, too.

But what makes the leaves turn to these fiery hues? Whether you consider the foliage display garish and loud, or soft and mellow, the effects are brought about by a combination of chemical reactions within the leaf cells. For the sake of simplicity, let us regard the leaves as the 'factories' of the plant. These factories, once subjected to sunlight, convert the water and food taken up by the roots, into energy – essential for good growth and development. This energy is then carried away to all parts of the plant's system.

At the end of the summer season, the great majority of plants – from trees a hundred feet tall to the prized plants in our garden borders – discard their leaves, but not before they withdraw from them as much of the goodness as they can, for storage in their stems or underground parts. This withdrawal causes the usual green colouring in the foliage to change to one of the many great and brilliant shades so characteristic of the autumn scene.

Our school botany lessons told us of the green colouring agent in plants – chlorophyll. While this is the most important of pigments, leaves and stems also contain a number of others, varying in colour and strength from plant to plant. During autumn these pigments accumulate and give the vivid colours – the strongest being those in the range of deep reds and purples. These strong colours occur best when the autumn days are mild

and sunny, and the nights cool and still. On the other hand, the pale yellow and orange tints enjoy warm, overcast, even thundery autumn weather.

Unlikely as it may seem, we can, on a small scale, actually improve the potential performance of the autumn tints in our own gardens. Once we accept that healthy leaves are the ones that colour best, all we have to do is follow a programme of good cultivation, and pest and disease control.

Where there is a poor soil, perhaps one that is extremely sandy and where all goodness is washed and drained through, or maybe on a new housing estate where the builders have systematically removed the valuable topsoil (and not replaced it), there are often poor, premature displays of autumn colour.

Leaf colour seems to develop more strongly on moisture retentive soils, preferably ones that contain a good quantity of organic material.

Once we have the chemical factor under control, we also have to contend with and battle against the climatic elements. Bad weather early in the growing season can damage young leaves, and so influence the eventual quality of the autumn display.

The richness of autumn, however, is not confined solely to that of leaf colour: there is also, of course, the abundance of fruits, which make some trees and shrubs invaluable. Unfortunately, these days it is not always easy to find good, wide-ranging displays of berries and seedheads.

There are a number of reasons why. In the country, the hedges are trimmed back to old wood before the fruits appear, and of those not trimmed Man robs wild brambles for

Two hollies together: *Ilex aquifolium* 'J.C.Van Tol' with red
berries, and 'Bacciflava' with yellow ones.

preserves, elderberries for wine and champagne, holly and mistletoe for indoor decoration, and so on. Human interference also has its effect in tidy, well-kept gardens: many plants are pruned or dead-headed after flowering (and rightly so if we are to encourage good flowers the following year, but at the expense of the autumn berries!).

We have already discussed the effect of the weather on leaf colour, but if sharp frosts or heavy winds affect the plants' flowers at setting time, there is every chance that the autumn fruits will be poor, in number as well as quality.

Then of course there are the banes of the gardener's life – marauding birds. To start with they generally go for the darker toned fruits, usually purple-black, but also including the many shades of red. These, I suspect, appear more 'ripe' to the bird. Certainly the lighter fruits (such as white snowberries or pink pernettyas) seem to be less attractive. Birds are not just fussy about the colour of their food, they like their berries to have a 'squashy' texture, too – the softest berries, such as those of brambles and elderberries, are usually the first to go. The harder fruits, like rose hips and holly, are generally left until a sharp frost has made them pulpy and more palatable.

Autumn fruits come in all shapes and sizes, from the tiny purple globes of *Callicarpa bodinieri giraldii* to the large, almost conical orange-red crab apples of *Malus* 'John Downie'.

The last area of colour to consider is that of the flower display. Summer is understandably the richest season for flowers, when everything from tall parkland trees to minuscule grass plants puts forth its floral offering. But autumn, too, has an abundant number of blooming beauties.

Consider the huge waxy, creamy blooms of *Magnolia grandiflora*, the blue offerings of *Ceanothus* 'Gloire de Versailles', the many shades of Michaelmas daisies and hardy cyclamen. Each has its own beauty and story to tell, making autumn far more than the depressing, misty period that comes between your summer holiday and the first snowfall of winter.

Autumn provides us with a rich pageant of colour, and it's up to us to make the most of it in our own gardens.

CHAPTER TWO

TREES IN AUTUMN

Few of us would deny that trees are important. In commerce they are essential for the everyday success of the human race – where would we be without paper? And now, after hundreds of years of felling, we are rather more sensible regarding conservation; tree plantations are springing up, where 30 years ago they were disappearing just as quickly. Natural woodlands, too, are again being allowed, and encouraged, to develop.

In heavily populated areas, street and park trees have been described as the 'lungs' of the city or town; as already mentioned, they throw out life-giving oxygen and take in carbon dioxide. In other areas of human well-being, it is an accepted fact that trees filter wind and noise, making life more physically bearable. Additionally, they break up the monotonous hard lines of buildings and screen unsightly views, so improving the aesthetic outlook.

In gardens we can regard the splendour of trees much more on a one-to-one basis, and we are able to appreciate their full beauty in close-up detail. Be it for foliage, fruit, flowers or shape, the tree forms the focal point in gardens of all sizes.

A word of warning, though. Where room and space are concerned, large forest trees like *Carpinus betulus* (hornbeam), *Acer pseudoplatanus* (sycamore) and *Tilia × europaea* (common lime), are best kept at a distance of 21 m (70 ft) from the nearest building: *Quercus robur* (common oak), *Populus nigra* 'Italica' (Lombardy poplar) and *Aesculus hippocastanum* (horse chestnut) 30 m (100 ft) away, while that common large *Salix babylonica* (weeping willow) should not be planted any closer than 45 m (150 ft) from foundations –

especially where the soil is clay.

Don't forget, too, that apart from their appearance, trees appeal to one of our other senses – hearing. In autumn, when the leaves are turning brittle, and when the seasonal winds are increasing, we can stand back and enjoy that frenzy of rustling. To me, the sound of the boughs being strained is bettered only by that of trickling water – but that's another story!

Sadly, in these days of small modern and town gardens there seems to be less and less room for a tree. Naturally, there are short trees and thin trees which can be considered with some success, and anybody with a plot of 4.5 × 4.5 m (15 x 15 ft) or more has room for a tree of some description. Of course, one could consider the fact that the smaller the plot, the more important a tree is, since if you are restricted in area, the only way to go – if you want good plant coverage – is up!

It's also comforting to remember that, although trees generally create varying amounts of shade – which the majority of popular garden flowers find difficult to accept – there are many extremely beautiful plants which actually require full or part shade. Also, in a vast number of instances trees are planted for the purpose of providing some shade, where we can sit out in comfort in high summer without being baked.

Though it may have little practical application, it is interesting to know that, of the thousands of tree species in cultivation, there are only 35 species native to Britain. These include *Juniperus communis* (common juniper), *Pinus sylvestris* (Scots pine), *Ulmus procera* (English elm) and *Taxus baccata* (common yew). The majority of other kinds popularly grown for their ornamental value come from North America, the Far East and Europe. The hot lands of Africa and Australasia have relatively little to offer.

Whatever type of tree you decide on, don't keep putting off planting it from year to year. Time means growth, and most trees need to put on a bit of size before they begin to show their true colours. Because of their size and potential, trees are among the first things that should be planted in a new garden so they do not lose a single season.

The following alphabetical section takes the form of a list of types recommended for their decorative value in autumn. Leaves and berries are the most colourful areas on which to concentrate, with flowers (which, where trees are concerned, are rare in autumn) and conifer foliage coming in third and fourth positions. One or more of these 40 or so trees will add a new, colourful dimension to your gardening scene.

ACER (MAPLE)

For brilliant autumn colouring, the maples are hard to beat. It's important to choose species and varieties to suit your particular garden, as some of these beauties can eventually attain 18m (60ft) in height, and take on the habit of a forest tree. On the other hand there are a few that make neat shrub-like miniatures. For the small garden forms of *A. japonicum* and *A. palmatum* (the Japanese maples) are generally the best. They are widely available in garden shops and, though they may seem expensive, they are a good investment. Most are hardy and are unfussy as to soil, though they tend to prefer a moist but well-drained positon rather than a dry one. When planting, try to position away from winds, draughts and exposure to the elements.

A. japonicum. A small tree growing to 6m (20ft) or so, with a spread of 2.4–3m (8–10ft). A slow grower, the shallowly lobed leaves turn from soft green to orange and fiery red. Two excellent varieties are 'Aconitifolium' (sharply lobed leaves which turn ruby red or crimson), and 'Vitifolium' (fan-shaped leaves changing to a brilliant red).

A. palmatum. The eventual height of this rounded tree could be 4.5m (15ft), with a spread of 2.4m (8ft). The pale to mid-green leaves have five or seven lobes. One of the best varieties on offer is 'Senkaki' (the coral bark maple). All of the younger branches are a conspicuous and attractive coral red, but the autumn leaves are a soft canary yellow.

A. platanoides (Norway maple). Rather large, this tree will reach a height of 9–10.5m (30–35ft), with a spread of 4.5–6m (15–20ft). It's a native of Europe, but not Britain, and one of the toughest, fastest growing and most popular of the larger kinds. The five-lobed leaves present an exquisitely colourful autumn display when they turn from their mid-green to golden yellow.

AMELANCHIER (SNOWY MESPILUS)

A small group of hardy small trees and shrubs. As well as their often rich autumn colours, these distant cousins of the rose produce abundant white flowers in spring, before the leaves are fully developed. Best soil conditions are moist, well-drained and lime-free.

A. canadensis (also seen as *A. lamarckii*). This is probably the best. It has a variety of common names, including Juneberry and shadbush. Height and spread: 3m (10ft). The mid-green leaves of summer actually start life in spring as coppery red, and finish in autumn as a blaze of orange and red.

CERCIDIPHYLLUM

A very small group of trees noted for their autumn colouring – the flowers are

Malus 'Golden Hornet', without doubt the best of the yellow-fruited crab apples.

insignificant. They are not fussy as to soil, but perform less satisfactorily on dry chalk soils. If yours is a cold exposed garden, it would be best not to include a cercidiphyllum, as its young growths are subject to injury by spring frosts.

C. japonicum. A height of 6–7.5ft (20–25ft), and a spread of 4.5–6m (15–20ft) can be reached. In autumn the rich leaves turn to a lemon-white flushed with a pastel pink, giving an overall effect of pale mauve.

CORNUS (DOGWOOD, CORNEL)

This is a relatively large group of deciduous trees and shrubs containing a wide selection of forms grown for all of the ornamental reasons – leaves, flowers, fruits and stems. These beauties must be sited in sun, or partial shade, if the autumn tints are to be enjoyed at their best.

C. florida (flowering dogwood). This will attain 3–4.5m (10–15ft) in height, with a spread of 6m (20ft) or more (consider it a large shrub, or well-branched tree), unless on a poor, chalky, shallow soil, The dark green leaves turn to brilliant shades of orange and scarlet in autumn.

C. nuttallii. A versatile beauty. The spring flowers are creamy white, becoming pink; the leaves turn to yellow, occasionally red in autumn. Eventual height of this noble tree is 4.5–6m (15–20ft), with a spread of 2.4–3m (8–10ft).

CORYLUS (HAZEL)

As well as the autumn colouring, this group of trees is grown for its attractive male catkins and edible nuts. Hazelnuts (or cob-nuts) and filberts come under this botanical heading, and can be grown with some success in small gardens. Choose a sunny site, away from easterly winds.

C. avellana (hazelnut). Autumn is certainly the season for reaping the benefits. The nuts

ripen then, and the leaves turn a golden yellow. A height of 6m (20ft) may be reached, while the spread is as much as 4.5m (15ft); indeed, a dense thicket of erect stems is produced.

COTONEASTER

Where does one start with this huge group of attractive evergreen and deciduous trees and shrubs? All have small, white or pink flowers in late spring, usually followed by conspicuous autumn berries; all are extremely hardy, and easy to grow. The evergreen types are useful for hedging and screening; creeping kinds are suitable for ground-covering purposes, and more importantly, here, the deciduous kinds have rich autumn tints. Most are shrubs, but there are several tree-like specimens.

C. 'Cornubia'. Laden throughout autumn and winter with heavy crops of bright red berries accompanying comparatively large semi-evergreen leaves. Height and spread: 6m (20ft).

C. 'Hybridus Pendulus'. Usually available as a grafted, gracefully weeping tree. Overall height is 2.1–2.7m (7–9ft), with a spread of 1.5m (5ft). The weeping shoots reach down to ground level, and are clothed in glossy, evergreen leaves. The brilliant red autumn berries are quite spectacular.

CRATAEGUS (THORN)

Excellent in town, country and seaside areas, the thorns are often considered to be a group of unwieldy trees. Usually small, they are very hardy, and when established are tolerant of dry or very wet soils. White, pink or red flowers appear in spring or summer and, in a few cases, are followed by attractive berries.

C. monogyna (common hawthorn, May or quickthorn). A height of 9m (30ft) and a spread of 6m (20ft) can be reached with this

Parrotia persica (Persian ironwood), with autumn leaf tints of
yellow, orange, red and purple.

British tree. Leaf colouring is, depending on the season, not spectacular, but the red 'haws' or berries are a good seasonal feature. **C. prunifolia.** A compact, broad-leaved thorn with a height and spread of 4.5–6m (15–20ft). It is notable for its persistent, showy large red fruits, and polished oval leaves which turn to fiery orange-red in autumn.

EUCRYPHIA

There are not too many plants that produce flowers during the autumn months, but this small group of trees is well known for its late summer and autumn floral displays. They thrive in any moist but well-drained soil and resent dry soils, so should never be planted where the soil around the root area is exposed to the sun.

E. glutinosa. This is an excellent and versatile small tree, with a height of around 3m (10ft), and a spread of 1.8–2.4m (6–8ft). In high summer prominent white flowers are produced at the ends of the shoots, and in autumn the foliage ignites to shades of orange-red.

E. × nymansensis 'Nymansay'. Its flowers are its main feature. The dark, evergreen leaves are crowded in autumn with pure white, yellow-stamened flowers. Height: 4.5m (15ft). Spread: 1.8–2.4m (6–8ft).

FAGUS (BEECH)

Small gardens will not be able to accommodate any of the best fagus species, which is a great pity because they are superb autumn colourers. Fagus is only a small genus of trees, but it contains several of the most impressive, hardy, large deciduous trees in the northern hemisphere. Any soil will do, but some of the best trees are seen on the chalk downs of southern England.

F. sylvatica (common beech). It is a magnificent giant, from bud-break in spring when the green appears, until leaf-fall in autumn, when the foliage provides us with a period of gold. Height and spread: 12m (40ft).

F. sylvatica purpurea (purple beech). A collective name for a number of coloured-leaved forms, their foliage ranging from black-purple to copper during summer, changing in autumn to lighter shades of copper and bronzy crimson. Same size as the type.

GINKGO (MAIDENHAIR TREE)

A tree of great ornamental, botanical and even geographical interest. It is a distant relation to the conifer, yet is a broad-leaved tree, the sole survivor of an ancient plant family known to have existed 160 000 000 years ago. It is perfectly hardy, and thrives in most soils. The ginkgo has only really been studied deeply in the last century. The first known cultivated specimen was transplanted to the Royal Botanic Gardens at Kew in 1761, after the death of the tree's owner, the Duke of Argyll. It was a wall plant for a number of years, grown against a boiler-house until 1860, when the building was demolished. Perhaps as a result of those early days, the tree is now shapeless, sprawling and divided into three stems almost from ground level. This may be the oldest known specimen, but it is not the nicest, nor the tallest. As far as expected heights are concerned, it is an unpredictable tree. Two specimens have been recorded at 22.5m (75ft) and 20.6m (62ft) – both are branchy and columnar, and over 100 years old. It is probably safe to say that *eventually* the ginkgo will reach a height of 15–21m (50–70ft), with a spread of 6–9m (20–30ft). But, having said this, after 20 or 30 years (the maximum period for which the planter of such a tree can be reasonably expected to be interested in its dimensions), the tree may be only 9m (30ft) in height, with a spread of 4.5–6m (15–20ft).

G. biloba. The fan-shaped leaves are like

Characteristic autumn leaves of the scarlet oak,
Quercus coccinea 'Splendens'.

Orange, scarlet and gold: *Rhus typhina* (stag's horn sumach).

From one of the most popular groups of small garden trees, this is
the white-berried *Sorbus hupehensis*.

large versions of the tender maidenhair fern (hence the common name). They turn a beautiful clear yellow before falling in autumn.

GLEDITSIA

A small group of trees which have a formidable armour of vicious large spines. Related distantly to garden peas and beans, their insignificant greenish flowers are succeeded by unattractive seed pods. The leaves are its main attraction; they are divided into leaflets and are a fresh, light green shade.

G. triacanthos 'Sunburst' (golden honey locust). Undoubtedly the best form: it has bright yellow foliage which turns buttery in autumn – and it's thornless! It deserves to be planted with a dark background to display the leaves at their best; it makes a superb lawn specimen. Height: 4.5–6m (15–20ft). Spread: 4.5m (15ft).

ILEX (HOLLY)

The many forms of holly are invaluable for garden decoration. They have a reputation of being old-fashioned, even Victorian (inferring that they are dark, dull and sombre), but with careful selection, you can have a variety of hollies which are not only bright in leaf, but also in berry and bark. They can be tolerant of polluted city air, or of salt-laden coastal air. They are excellent subjects for planting in hedges (also affording some degree of protection – their thick, often impenetrable foliage can be a real deterrent to the opportunist thief!). In order to obtain the often highly colourful berries, trees of both sexes must be present, as male and female flowers are generally borne on different trees. In areas where there are already a number of hollies growing, there should be no problem. There are a great many forms with variegated leaves. These can be yellow-edged, silver-edged, golden-blotched, marbled, and so on.

But it is the quantity and quality of end-of-season berries which interest us here.

I × altaclarensis 'Golden King'. In spite of its name this is a female variety, and has gold-margined oval leaves and bright red berries. It reaches a height of 9m (30ft), with a spread of 6m (20ft).

I. aquifolium 'Bacciflava' (yellow fruited holly). The common name spells it out. Here we have a really handsome tree 5.4m (18ft) high, with a spread of 4.5m (15ft), with dark green spiny leaves and bright yellow berries.

I. aquifolium 'J.C. Van Tol'. An outstanding variety, and probably the best of the fruiting kinds, with large red berries. It will reach 5.4m (18ft) in height, with a spread of 1.8–3m (6–10ft).

● One holly which you are unlikely to come across is the fabled white-berried form. This was first heard of in the early 1700s, and last mentioned in a list around 1915. Recent reported sightings have come to nothing. Keep your eyes peeled!

KOELREUTERIA (GOLDENRAIN TREE)

A small group of deciduous trees, originally from China. They are recommended as being easy to grow: they are not fussy as to soil or site, but they do give of their best (as regards flowering and autumn colour) when there is a hot, dry summer. Do not confuse the common name with that of the laburnum (golden rain).

K. paniculata. The large ferny leaves, which open red in spring, change to a soft mid-green for summer, and turn a rich golden amber in autumn. The summer flowers are sometimes followed by peculiar bladder-like green fruits, flushed with red. Height: 5.4m (18ft). Spread: 3m (10ft).

LIQUIDAMBAR (SWEET GUM)

The woodlands of North America provide

Sorbus 'Joseph Rock', with its cream yellow berries
and fiery leaves.

Orange, red and yellow autumn leaf tints of
Stewartia pseudocamellia.

some of the world's richest autumn colouring. One tree native to that continent, and which plays a very large part in the scene, is the liquidambar. It grows naturally on swampy ground, and in cultivation performs best in a moist, non-chalky soil of reasonable quality. In Britain it doesn't always colour fully, but a tree planted near open water is always attractive, and most years it will end with a spectacular pyramid of orange and crimson.

L. styraciflua (sweet gum, red gum). It is a slender tree, reaching a height of 7.5m (25ft), and a spread of 3.6m (12ft). If you have room for just one tree of this size, let it be a liquidambar – you will not be disappointed. In winter the naked stems reveal attractive corky bark; tiny green flowers appear in spring, and the maple-like leaves, which are glossy bright green all summer, turn to their fiery hues in autumn. This tree is often confused with the acers (maples), but the way the leaves are arranged alternately on the branches easily identifies it. Also, sweet gum leaves, when crushed, have a pleasant eucalyptus-like smell.

LIRIODENDRON (TULIP TREE)

Another tree from North America, and every bit as interesting as the liquidambar. It's hardy and fast-growing, will thrive in most soils (including chalk), but prefers a deep, moist well-drained loam.

L. tulipifera. The four-lobed, saddle-shaped leaves of this tree are attractive at all times, but in autumn they change from their light green to gorgeous shades of butter yellow. The common name refers to the peculiar tulip-like yellowish green summer flowers. Height: 7.5m (25ft). Spread: 4.5m (15ft). The form 'Aureomarginatum' is worth a special mention: it is a striking form in which the leaves possess a wide border of yellow, brighter in spring and becoming yellowish green in early autumn.

MAGNOLIA

There are few hardy trees or shrubs with blooms so large and so breathtaking as the magnolias. And it's not too often that one comes across exotic autumn tree flowers. Here we have one that comes into both categories. Magnolias are a useful and variable bunch; most will tolerate heavy clay soils and atmospheric pollution.

M. grandiflora. A magnificent evergreen species, generally grown as a wall shrub, although it's not a climber. The large, leathery glossy leaves are clothed on the underside with rust-coloured hairs when young. It is the beauty of flower which makes it an important entry here. The enormous creamy white blooms, which have a delicious lemon-like fragrance, appear from late summer, often until the depths of winter. The only disappointment is that this tree does not generally offer a great mass of flowers at any one time. Instead they appear in ones and twos over the long season. But individually, the blooms have a fascinating beauty. A height, in completely favourable conditions, of 4.5–6m (15–20ft) can be achieved, with a spread of around 3m (10ft).

MALUS (FLOWERING CRABS)

The most popular flowering trees for general garden cultivation are prunus (flowering cherries), and malus. Each lights up our gardens in spring with white, red and pink blossoms. The beauty of the malus group, however, is not confined to the flowers and fruits. The latter are often large, colourful and suitable for wine- and jelly-making (after all, the genus includes the great range of edible dessert and culinary apples). Several of the crabs offer autumn leaf tints too. As far as conditions are concerned, enrich the soil with peat or well-rotted compost before planting. All of the following trees are normally sold as standards with 90–180cm (3–

6ft) clear stems; when grown as bushes they are much less effective.

M.'Golden Hornet'. This is, without doubt, the best of the yellow-fruited crabs. The white spring blooms are replaced by rich golden yellow round fruits which clothe the branches in clusters. A height of 5.4m (18ft) can be reached, while a spread of 3–4.5m (10–15ft) is normal.

M. tschonoskii. Certainly the best crab for the brilliance of its autumn leaves. They are mid-green during summer and felted with grey hairs beneath. In autumn, however, they are transformed into shades of yellow, orange, purple and red. As a bonus there are, of course, the 'multicoloured' round fruits (they go through stages of yellowish green tinged with reddish purple). This tree will reach a great height for apples: 10.5m (35ft). With a spread of only 3m (10ft), though, it is an upright species.

METASEQUOIA (DAWN REDWOOD)

The fascinating story of this tree has been told many times. It is a prehistoric coniferous – but deciduous – tree, bearing fine, flat pale green needle-like leaves. Until 1941, when a growing specimen was discovered in a Chinese temple, all that was known about this tree was gleaned from fossils.

M. glyptostroboides. The first specimens to be planted in Britain are now 15–18m (50–60ft) high, and 6m (20ft) across. A moist soil is essential, near water preferred – which unfortunately makes this tree somewhat out of the reach of the average gardener. Before the foliage falls in late autumn we are treated to gorgeous rust-red tints.

NYSSA (TUPELO)

A small group of trees which contains one of the finest specimens for autumn colour. It's a slow-growing tree from the eastern USA. A

damp, loamy soil suits it best. Once established, nyssas resent disturbance, so they should be planted as young as possible, and then left.

N. sylvatica. Reaching a height of around 6m (20ft), it spreads out to about 3m (10ft). In ideal conditions the normally glossy dark green foliage exhibits a glorious array of scarlet, red and orange in autumn.

PARROTIA (PERSIAN IRONWOOD)

This is a useful woodland tree originally from the Middle East. It is mainly grown for its rich autumn colour, but it does produce small curious flowers (which have red stamens but no petals) in late winter. In addition, the bark on older trees flakes away, leaving small patches of green, grey and brown. This patterned effect is best seen if the lower branches are removed. Any well-drained loamy soil will suit this attractive tree.

P. persica. It will reach 6m (20ft) or more, with a spread of 3–4.5m (10–15ft). The long, glossy green leaves turn bright yellow, orange-red and purple in autumn.

PRUNUS

A large group, and perhaps the most widely planted ornamental trees. This is a varied genus which includes some familiar, and quite distinct, plant groups: almonds, cherries, laurels, peaches and plums. As a group they are not fussy as to soil as long as it's not waterlogged; many of the spring-flowering Japanese cherries actually thrive on shallow chalk soils. A sunny spot is preferred, but partial shade will not be a problem.

P.'Kanzan'. The most widely seen Japanese cherry. It has a height and spread of around 9m (30ft). Perhaps more noted for its profuse display of large, double purplish pink blooms in spring, it also gives a good account of itself in autumn, with yellow and orange leaves.

P. sargentii. A Japanese cherry with single

One of the red Japanese maples: *Acer palmatum* 'Dissectum
Atropurpureum' (*centre & right mid-picture*).

pink spring flowers and attractive dark chestnut brown bark (a good winter feature). It's a rounded tree, reaching a height of 7.8m (26ft), and a spread the same, if not more. As autumn approaches it's one of the first trees, and certainly the first cherry, to change colour. Glorious tints of orange and maroon are the order of the day.

P. spinosa (blackthorn, sloe). A small tree 3.9m (13ft) tall and across, often seen growing wild in the hedgerows. It's an early autumn colourer, transforming its mid-green leaves to pale butter yellow. The variety 'Purpurea' has purple-red leaves which turn to bronze.

QUERCUS (OAK)

As ornamental trees, the oaks have much to offer although, sadly, many are too big for today's average garden. With their massive frames, domed heads, wavy-edged leaves and glossy acorns in cups they are a stately part of our countryside. The majority are hardy and suitable for most soils and situations. Despite the many variations in leaf shape, colour and acorn habit, the oaks have unmistakable family traits – large size, longevity and a dislike of shallow soils.

Q. coccinea (scarlet oak). A relatively fast-growing tree when young, reaching an ultimate height of 7.5–9m (25–30ft), and a spread of 4.5–6m (15–20ft). A lime-free soil is preferred by this particular oak. The large, sharply lobed leaves are glossy green, turning to rich scarlet. The autumn tinting often develops in patches, almost branch by branch, and can last well into the winter. The form 'Splendens' is generally accepted to be more reliably colourful.

Q. rubra (red oak). One of the most impressive of all hardy trees, reaching the same sort of proportions as the scarlet oak. The drooping, coarsely lobed dull green leaves turn a tawny orange in early autumn, changing to brown before they fall.

RHUS (SUMACH)

Some of the most architecturally beautiful trees are included in this small genus. All provide excellent autumnal colour, even in towns and cities (they are pollution-tolerant). Suckers may occur but rather than regard them as troublesome, during autumn carefully lift them and replant. They are excellent propagation material.

R. typhina (stag's horn sumach). Height: 3.6–4.5m (12–15ft). Spread: 3.6–4.8m (12–16ft). The candelabra-like branches are gaunt while the bush is small but eventually become well-furnished and flat-topped. The pointed leaves change to fiery orange-scarlet, tinged with scarlet and gold. Unfortunately they soon fall, but they then leave curiously felted stems which are not without interest. The variety 'Laciniata' is as colourful, but with attractively cut ferny leaves.

SORBUS (WHITEBEAM, MOUNTAIN ASH)

The most popular small garden trees are the species of prunus (flowering cherries). Next come the malus (crab apples) and then, in third place, we have trees from the sorbus genus. Part of their fame is due to the variety of attractions they offer: white flowers in late spring/early summer, rich autumn leaf tints, and an abundance of brightly coloured berries. All species within the group are hardy and deciduous, and tolerant of a wide range of soils and situations.

S. aria (whitebeam). An extremely tough tree native to Britain. It reaches a height of 4.5–6m (15–20ft), and a spread of 3–4.5m (10–15ft). Its rounded leaves are covered by brilliant white felt in spring, changing to grey-green and white-backed in summer, finally to beige-gold in autumn, when they are joined by bunches of deep crimson berries.

S. aucuparia (mountain ash, rowan). This

The small, bright red berries of *Berberis thunbergii*.

Bright blue berries, each set in a crimson star-shaped calyx, are the main attraction of *Clerodendrum trichotomum fargesii*.

tree will attain a height of 9m (30ft), with a spread of 6m (20ft). The leaves are divided into numerous sharply toothed leaflets – quite different from the whitebeam. Its autumn leaves are not particularly worthy, but this is usually the first sorbus to ripen its berries when, in late summer/early autumn, they turn a bright orange-red. Unfortunately blackbirds have a liking for these rich-coloured fruits, so it may be advisable to grow the paler-berried variety 'Xanthocarpa', with orange-yellow fruits.

S. 'Embley'. A vigorous, erect-branched tree when young. An overall height of 10.5m (35ft), and a spread of 7.5m (25ft). The scarlet autumn leaves accompany orange-red berries: quite a spectacle!

S. hupehensis. Height: 6m (20ft). Spread: 3.6m (12ft). White or pink-tinged berries are carried in loose, drooping clusters well into winter.

S. 'Joseph Rock'. A graceful, narrow tree often reaching a height of 9m (30ft), and a spread of 4.5m (15ft). Leaves turn to a fiery combination of orange, red, copper and purple, while the berries deepen from cream to golden yellow. They last well after the leaves have disappeared, and birds seem to ignore them, unless it's a particularly cold season.

STEWARTIA (Syn. STUARTIA)

A small group of deciduous trees and shrubs, whose garden appeal lies in their peeling bark (a good winter attraction), showy white summer flowers and autumn colour. All appreciate a moist but well-drained, lime-free, non-exposed site.

S. pseudocamellia. A small Japanese tree reaching 6m (20ft) in height and 4.5m (15ft) across. The rich orange, red and yellow autumn leaf tints are a perfect foil to the bark which flakes into patterns of cream, bright green and fawn-grey.

TAXODIUM (SWAMP CYPRESS)

Similar to *Metasequoia glyptostroboides* in performance and habit, but not as large. It's a deciduous conifer, with only one species in general cultivation. It grows well in most types of soil, but really thrives in those which are too wet for any other tree.

T. distichum. A mature specimen will reach 10.5m (35ft) in height, and 4.5m (15ft) across. In autumn, before the needles fall, it makes a breathtaking column of fine rusty brown, harmonizing with the fibrous red-brown bark.

CHAPTER THREE

SHRUBS AND CLIMBERS IN AUTUMN

In Victorian times shrubs tended to be planted in dark, dense shrubberies, which did not allow them to be seen at their best. We are better informed today, and our gardens are planted up with more feeling, with more consideration to the ultimate heights and habits of our shrubs. They are, after all, the mainstay of almost every garden.

Many 'casual' gardeners are of the opinion that once shrubs have flowered, they are dull for the rest of the year, providing plain, uninteresting greenery. These comments are perhaps made against subjects such as rhododendrons, lilacs and philadelphuses, without taking into account the vast range of variations in size and colour. There are also many shrubs which have more than just the one season of interest. Consider the spring foliage, summer flowers, autumn berries and leaf tints, and winter twigs.

In gardening terms shrubs are far more common than trees or conifers, due mainly to the fact that most trees are too large for the average garden, and conifers produce no flower display, with little variation in year-round foliage colour.

All too often modern gardens are flat and regular in shape so, along with trees if there is sufficient room, the first task in a new garden should be to give life and interest by introducing different shapes, heights and colours in the shrubs we choose. And, after all, shrubs can be put to a great many uses in the garden. They can be grown to cover the ground and help smother weeds; a number can fill a bed or border to make a larger display; individual shrubs can be sited as solitary specimens, and they can be planted close to – and adorn – house walls, to break up the hard building lines. One thing shrubs cannot be expected to do is to grow upwards more than, say, 4.5m (15ft). If you desire something higher than this you will have to choose a tree, suitable conifer or wall climber.

Although quite different from conventional shrubs, climbing plants are included in this chapter. These are invaluable for softening bleak concrete walls and furnishing hard brick surfaces. The use of climbers is also recommended over arches and pergolas, and along fences. There are relatively few with autumn merit, but those that do come within the scope of this book really are quite spectacular.

The most popular shrubs are those clothed with green leaves for the greater part of the year, and with attractive blooms for a relatively shorter period. Regular coloured foliage can be just as important as the display of flowers; yellow, purple, coppery or variegated leaves on evergreen shrubs give us colour all year round.

However, we are more interested here in shrubs with autumn leaf tints. These often outshine any floral display. Add to these the numerous types which add colour by producing an abundant display of fruits and seed-pods, and we can see that there is an almost infinite variety of shrubs from which to choose.

In Britain the climate makes it possible to grow shrubs from almost every country in the world, e.g. camellias and rhododendrons from China and Japan can be grown with brooms from Spain and North Africa; *Ulex europaeus* (gorse) from the Scottish moors often jostles for space with the striking *Embothrium coccineum* (Chilean firebush).

One of the shrubby veronicas with autumn flowers and decorative
leaves: *Hebe* × *andersonii* 'Variegata'.

With shrubs, and to a certain degree trees, one should consider the proportion of ever-green and deciduous types to be planted, according to one's requirements. Also think about the light and shade effects upon other occupants of the garden. Because of the variety on offer, when putting these thoughts into operation one has to be discriminating, almost to the point of ruthlessness. To a degree I have experienced this when compiling the A-Z list of shrubs which follows – to me it was more a case of what to leave out than what to include. Nevertheless, the 50 or so shrubs recommended here are a good indication of the variety available.

Growing shrubs is one of the easiest – and most rewarding – aspects of gardening. You won't go far wrong if you choose sensibly, plant properly and prune correctly. The most common problems occur when shrubs are planted too close together, and when they are pruned in the wrong way or at the wrong time. Become clear on these practices and you will enjoy a permanent garden feature which will give delight for years.

ABELIA

There are relatively few shrubs which flower during the autumn months, so this is a welcome sight (not that we are deprived of colour when there are so many leaf tints to enjoy). Abelias are easy to grow, even in cold districts if they are give a sheltered spot. Light, loamy soils are best, but any free-draining soil will produce satisfactory growth.

A. × grandiflora. This is the form to go for if autumn flowers are desired. It's a vigorous grower, and usually evergreen (although each year many of the glossy dark green leaves will fall). The flowers come in the form of small pink and white trumpets, starting in mid-summer and persisting until mid-autumn. A height and spread of up to 1.8 m (6 ft) can be expected.

ACER (MAPLE)

We have already looked at some of the tree maples (p.12), but there are shrubby, low-growing types as well.

A. palmatum 'Dissectum'. The leaves are very deeply cut and finely divided, green in summer and scarlet in autumn. It is such a slow grower that after 10 years it may have only reached a little more than 1 m (3½ft). Its ultimate height and spread will be nearer 1.8 m (6 ft).

A. palmatum 'Dissectum Atropurpureum'. Same size of shrub, and similarly shaped leaves, but with quite a different foliage colour. The leaves are purple in summer, turning to crimson as they age.

AZALEA

Botanically, deciduous azaleas should be classed as rhododendron, but in general garden terms the two are considered separately. These versatile shrubs are famed equally for their riot of flower colour in spring, and their leaf colour in autumn. They may be grown in a moist yet well-drained soil provided no free lime is present: almost all are lime-haters. They will tolerate atmospheric pollution, making them ideal for town gardens. Apart from the removal of the dead flower heads in summer, no regular pruning is required. Deciduous azaleas can be divided into several groups:

Ghent hybrids. These are the tallest, with a height of 1.8–2.4 m (6–8ft) and a spread of 1.5–2.4 m (5–8 ft). Small, scented, honey-suckle-like flowers appear in late spring. 'Corneille' has creamy spring flowers and superb golden foliage in autumn. 'Raphael de Smet' produces rose-coloured blooms flushed with white in spring, followed by yellow foliage in autumn.

Knap Hill azaleas. Larger, brilliantly coloured, trumpet-shaped blooms. The height attained is around 1.5–2.1 m (5–7 ft), with a

A fine example of *Parthenocissus tricuspidata* 'Veitchii' (Boston ivy), clinging to brickwork.

spread of 1.5–2.4m (5–8ft). For good autumn colour look for 'Klondyke'. The young foliage is bronze-red, turning to green, and ending up butter yellow before falling. The spring blooms are golden yellow, flushed red.

Mollis azaleas. This type produces large unscented blooms before the leaves appear in spring. A height of 1.2–1.8m (4–6ft), with a spread of 1.5–2.4m (5–8ft) may be reached. Look for the variety 'Christopher Wren', a compact bush with deep orange-yellow spring flowers and bronze autumn leaves.

BERBERIS (BARBERRY)

Tremendous range of colour and form is offered by this popular group of shrubs – there are well over 100 named forms in cultivation today. All are armed with sharp thorns, which is useful where intruders or vandals are common (such as parks and other public places). Open, sunny sites suit these shrubs, and any well-drained soil will do.

B. × 'Buccaneer'. A wonderful autumn shrub. The small soft-green leaves are transformed to a brilliant flame colour. Just as spectacular are the clusters of large crimson berries which last well into the winter.

B. thunbergii. This grows to little more than 1.5m (5ft) in height and spread. Pale yellow flowers light up the shrubs in spring. In autumn the fresh green foliage turns to brilliant red, accompanying small bright red berries. The variety 'Atropurpurea' has rich, reddish purple leaves throughout the season, increasing in intensity as autumn develops.

CALLICARPA

This is not often seen, and is sadly underrated. Its rarity is perhaps due to the effects a harsh winter has upon it. However, give it a sheltered spot in reasonable soil, and it should delight you for years.

C. bodinieri giraldii. Small lilac flowers are produced in mid-summer, but it is the quite remarkable profusion of pale purple berries, like small evenly coloured pearls, that appear from the beginning of autumn until early winter, which make this shrub stand out. Several are needed in close proximity for adequate pollination, however. The ultimate height and spread of this shrub is around 2.1m (7ft).

CAMELLIA

These are magnificent flowering evergreens, with shiny leaves almost as eye-catching as the blooms. The exotic, waxy flowers are rounded, and either single or double, depending on variety. White-flowered forms generally need more protection from the worst the winter can throw at them. Likewise, double-flowering varieties are not as hardy as the singles. A lime-free soil (or at least neutral) is required by these stately shrubs. The majority flower in winter and spring, but there is one species which blooms in autumn.

C. sasanqua **'Narumi-gata'.** The most reliable flowering variety of the species. Large, fragrant, creamy white blooms are produced from mid-autumn and appear off and on until early spring, especially if given the protection of a south or west-facing wall. Height and spread: 3–4.5m (10–15ft).

CARYOPTERIS (BLUE SPIRAEA)

An unusual group of shrubs originally from Eastern Asia. Unusual because they flower in late summer and autumn (most shrubs offer their blooms in spring and early summer), and because the blooms are of a delicate blue. If you live on a chalk soil, this shrub should do particularly well.

C. × clandonensis. The grey-green

Excellent against a wall, as a hedge, or by itself in a lawn, this
orange-berried firethorn is *Pyracantha coccinea* 'Lalandei'.

One of the best yellow-berried firethorns: *Pyracantha rogersiana* 'Flava'.

aromatic foliage is covered until mid-autumn with feathery clusters of bright blue blooms. The variety 'Ferndown' has darker, violet-blue flowers. One of the smallest shrubs so far covered, with an average height and spread of 60cm (2ft).

CEANOTHUS (CALIFORNIAN LILAC)

Of the few blue-flowering shrubs, ceanothus has to rate as one of the best. They look wonderful as specimen shrubs in a border or lawn and even better against the shelter of a wall. There are both deciduous and evergreen kinds. Unfortunately harsh winters can kill these North American bushes, but the more established your plant, the better chance of survival it will have. Any well-drained soil will do, except solid chalk.

C. 'Autumnal Blue'. This is an evergreen form, reaching a height and spread of 1.8–2.7m (6–9ft). Its rich blue blooms give a glorious display well into autumn.

C. × 'Gloire de Versailles'. With a height and spread of around 2.1m (7ft), this deciduous form provides us with powder blue flowers on long, arching stems.

CHAENOMELES (JAPONICA, FLOWERING QUINCE)

Being completely hardy, being able to thrive in any soil or situation, and having vividly coloured spring flowers with useful and decorative autumn fruits, this shrub must be the gardener's dream. The flowers can be pure white, pink, orange, salmon or red and are a welcome sight at the end of winter. But it is the autumn crop of fruits which interests us here.

C. speciosa (syn. *Cydonia speciosa*). These have a dense, spreading habit, about 3m (10ft) high and wide. The aromatic, yellow-green autumn fruits can be used for making jelly. Look for the form 'Simonii', with velvety deep red, double flowers in spring.

CLERODENDRUM

Summer flowers followed by autumn berries and leaf tints make this a very worthy garden shrub. It will thrive in any cultivated garden soil, and will soon become vigorous.

C. trichotomum fargesii. The bright blue berries, each set in a crimson star-shaped calyx, are the main attraction. A height and spread of 3–4.5m (10–15ft) can be expected.

CORNUS (DOGWOOD, CORNEL)

We have already looked at *C. florida* and *C. nuttallii*, both tree forms. There are a number of shrubby forms, too, all appreciating the same cultural conditions as their tree-like cousins.

C. kousa chinensis. A large shrub up to 3.6m (12ft) high, and with a spread of 2.4–3m (8–10ft). It produces eye-catching white bracts, red strawberry-like fruits and crimson autumn leaves. A relatively uncommon form, but undeservedly so.

COTINUS (SMOKE TREE)

This small group of shrubs is grown for its wispy flower heads (which give the appearance of smoke from a distance), and attractive leaves. Any well-drained garden soil will suit these rounded shrubs. Light, sandy soils, however, bring out the finest autumn leaf tints. These make an excellent addition to the garden, either in a mixed border or as specimen shrubs in a lawn.

C. coggygria. A height and spread of around 3m (10ft) can be expected when mature. The round, mid-green leaves turn to bright yellow in autumn. The variety 'Royal Purple' has rich purple leaves throughout spring and summer, gradually changing to various shades of light red in autumn.

COTONEASTER

We have already looked at two tree forms: *C. 'Cornubia'* and *C. 'Hybridus Pendulus'*. There are, however, a great many shrubby forms, two of which are worth special mention for their autumn berries.

C. conspicuus 'Decorus'. This fully evergreen form has a height and spread of only 60–90cm (2–3ft), making it suitable for any garden, especially on banks or a rock garden. Bright red, round berries hang in large bunches from early autumn.

C. lacteus. This, arguably, is the best evergreen in the genus. It will reach a height of 4.5m (15ft), and a spread of 2.4–3.6m (8–12ft). The abundant crimson berries are late to ripen, and last well into winter.

EUONYMUS (SPINDLE)

A group of widely different shrubs, both evergreen and deciduous. Variegated evergreen types provide some interest in winter (p.75), but the deciduous types supply much autumn colour in fruit and leaf. The often very showy lobed or winged berries last well into the winter months. The small early summer flowers are insignificant, and of little interest. These shrubs thrive in practically any soil, and are quite at home on chalk.

E. alatus (winged spindle tree). Originally from the Far East, this beauty will reach an eventual height and spread of 1.8–2.4m (6–8ft). It is a slow grower, with characteristic corky wings on the branches. Curiously, the intensity of autumn leaf tints varies according to the situation: in full sun the leaves turn to crimson, in shade they change to pale yellow.

E. europaeus (spindle tree). This species is well known for its green wood, brilliant autumn leaf colour and rose red seed capsules enclosing orange seeds. Height: around 3m (10ft). Spread: 1.8–3m (6–10ft). The

form 'Red Cascade' makes a good, bushy head of leaves and provides a goodly quantity of fruits which hang below the branches from early autumn onwards.

FOTHERGILLA

A small group of North American shrubs, related to the instantly recognizable hamamelis (witch hazel). However, their main claim to fame is the intensity of the autumn colours. Of secondary value, the quite attractive spring flowers have no petals, but comprise numerous long, cream stamens in bottle-brush-like spikes. As with rhododendrons, a lime-free soil is best.

F. major. The broad dark green spring and summer leaves have a silvery sheen underneath. In autumn they assume orange-yellow or red tints. Height: 1.8–2.4m (6–8ft). Spread: 1.2–1.8m (4–6ft).

F. monticola. Very similar to, and often confused with *F. major*. This species is slightly larger: height 1.8–2.4m (6–8ft), spread 1.5–2.4m (5–8ft), and the green leaves do not possess the silver undersides. Various shades of red and orange are produced in autumn.

HAMAMELIS (WITCH HAZEL)

Witch hazels are popular garden shrubs for their winter flowers. The blooms, mainly yellow, are long-lasting, sweet-smelling and frost-resistant, making them some of the most valuable of winter shrubs. A sunny or partially shaded spot is appreciated, but you must give these shrubs room to spread. A lime-free loamy soil is preferred. The majority have acceptable autumn leaf tints.

H. × intermedia. A fairly strong growing hybrid form, with a height and spread of around 1.8–3m (6–10ft). The large winter blooms are spectacular but so is the autumn foliage, particularly in the form 'Jelena'

If male and female plants are grown together, *Viburnum davidii* produces small turquoise berries in autumn.

A climber with excellent autumn leaf colour: *Vitis coignetiae*
(Japanese crimson glory vine).

(shades of orange, bronze and red), and 'Ruby Glow' (yellow, flushed red).

H. japonica (Japanese witch hazel). A height and spread of 2.4–3m (8–10ft). The leaves of all forms are yellow, flushed with red.

H. mollis (Chinese witch hazel). Slightly smaller, this has a height and spread of 1.8–2.4m (6–8ft). The leaves here generally turn to butter yellow.

HEBE (SHRUBBY VERONICA)

A large group of evergreen shrubs, mainly originating from New Zealand. The glossy deep green leaves are one attraction of the hebe, and a number of species are neat and compact, making them ideal for use as ground cover plants. A well drained soil is best, but hebes grow well in most gardens. In cities they withstand grime and dust; in coastal gardens they tolerate salty winds. However, in cold exposed gardens a prolonged winter may damage plants beyond repair. There are two forms worth mentioning for their autumn flowers.

H. × andersonii 'Variegata'. A very decorative shrub 90–150cm (3–5ft) in height and spread. The long flower spikes, starting off as pale mauve, soon fading to near-white, appear from late summer until late autumn. The mid-green leaves are edged with cream.

_H._ 'Autumn Glory'. Perhaps more dramatic in colour, this form produces a mound covered with spikes of violet blooms which last well into winter. Height and spread 60–90cm (2–3ft).

HIPPOPHAE (SEA BUCKTHORN)

This shrub is well suited to exposed and windy situations, making it a common subject for coastal gardens. Any ordinary well-drained soil will do.

H. rhamnoides. The leaves, which are silvery grey, fall in autumn to expose an abundance of orange-yellow berries. These, it appears, are ignored by birds. A height and spread of 2.4–3m (8–10ft) can be expected. This, and the fact that quite fierce thorns are produced, means that a large garden – where the shrub can be given a wide berth, yet still examined at close quarters – is more suitable.

HYPERICUM (ST JOHN'S WORT)

These shrubs will withstand dry soil conditions and grow freely in virtually all but waterlogged gardens. Many seem to spread well under trees or in sites where light and moisture is deficient. All hypericums produce bright flowers, varying in shade from cream to near-orange, depending on variety. A couple worth mentioning flower well into autumn.

_H._ 'Hidcote'. Probably the largest and showiest form, this reaches a height and spread of around 1.8m (6ft) in ideal conditions. Quite hardy, it produces masses of large golden yellow flowers until mid-autumn.

H. × inodorum 'Elstead'. This form is smaller, with a height of 90–120cm (3–4ft), and a spread of 1.2–1.8m (4–6ft). The flowers are smaller, too, but to compensate there are clusters of bright salmon red berries and purplish leaf tints. Unfortunately this form seems prone to the debilitating rust disease, but this should not put you off growing it.

LESPEDEZA (BUSH CLOVER)

Not as frequently seen as it deserves, this distant relative of the runner bean is extremely valuable where autumn flowers are required. The best site is in full sun and in a medium to light soil. You may experience difficulty in finding a nursery with this for sale, but it will certainly be worth the search.

L. thunbergii. Weeping branches carry trusses of rose pink pea flowers throughout autumn. A height of 2.1 m (7 ft), with a spread of 1.5 m (5 ft) may be attained. For best effect, plant this as a specimen shrub in a lawn.

LEYCESTERIA (PHEASANT BERRY)

A vigorous, extremely easy shrub to grow, the leycesteria gets its common name from the autumn berries which, in country areas, are attractive to pheasants. Any site will do, but more summer flowers – and consequently autumn berries – are produced on plants in sunny spots. Hard winter frosts may cause damage to the branches, but these will be renewed from the base in spring.

L. formosa. The most commonly grown species. Tiny white flowers are covered by hanging claret-coloured bracts throughout summer. These are followed by round, purple-black berries. Height and spread: 1.5–1.8 m (5–6 ft).

PARTHENOCISSUS (VIRGINIA CREEPER, BOSTON IVY)

The first of the climbing plants to be covered here. Confusion reigns over the naming of some plants in this genus. Instead, should they be known as ampelopsis or vitis? Which is the true Virginia creeper? Even distinguished botanists find it difficult to agree over the naming, but luckily for us home gardeners, all of the species are freely available, and a good nursery will not sell a specimen which has a doubtful name or habit. Contrary to popular belief, these do not create problems with house structures – they merely cling on to the cladding, not digging deep into the brickwork with damaging root systems. The ideal soil is a rich, loamy one with plenty of available moisture.

P. henryana (Chinese Virginia creeper). This will spread over a wall from its base to around 9 m (30 ft). The leaves come in groups of three or five; they are dark green during summer, changing to brilliant red in autumn. This is best if given a south or west-facing position.

P. quinquefolia (true Virginia creeper). The leaflets here are arranged to look like five fingers. They turn to brilliant crimson at the end of summer. The outward spread could be as much as 21 m (70 ft) from the base; indeed, very often pruning is required to keep its growth within limits.

P. tricuspidata 'Veitchii' (Boston ivy). This has crimson autumn leaves, slightly smaller than the true Virginia creeper. The outward spread is less, too, at around 15 m (50 ft) from the base.

PYRACANTHA (FIRETHORN)

This large group of shrubs has so many uses in the garden; abundant fluffy white flowers are produced in summer, huge clusters of berries hang in autumn and winter, and the green leaves clothe the stems all year round. Pyracanthas are often grown against walls where they enjoy a little shelter; they also appear as specimen plants in lawns, and are most suited to being planted as hedging material. Any well-drained, reasonably fertile soil will do. Practically all forms produce highly coloured berries (their main reason for being included here), but there are a few forms worth a special mention.

P. atalantioides. A vigorous shrub with glossy deep green leaves, and crimson autumn berries. Height and spread: 3–4.5 m (10–15 ft). The form 'Aurea' has deep yellow berries.

P. coccinea. An excellent upright species with the same dimensions as *P. atalantioides*, its pointed, mid-green leaves accompany bright red berries. The form 'Lalandei' has broader leaves and orange-red fruits.

P. rogersiana. This is slightly shorter, with an expected height of 3 m (10 ft), and a spread of up to 4.5 m (15 ft). Narrow mid-green leaves jostle for space with orange-red

In autumn the orange seed pods of *Physalis alkekengi franchetii*
(Chinese lantern) are revealed.

berries. Better is the bright yellow-berried form 'Flava'.

ROSA (ROSE)

It's difficult to know exactly which section should include our common garden hybrid tea and floribunda roses. As they are closer to shrubs than perennials, I'm including them here. While many roses bloom right through summer and autumn, it must be admitted that some perform better later in the year than others. Yellow and orange varieties seem, for some inexplicable reason, to survive into the autumn months better than most. Ramblers are, of course, summer-flowering, and some climbers are recurrent, flowering at intervals until winter.

Of the hybrid tea (large-flowered bush) range, the following are recommended for their autumn blooms: 'Adolf Horstmann' (bronze-yellow, edged pink), 'Alpine Sunset' (creamy yellow, flushed peach pink), 'Fragrant Cloud' (bright red), 'Just Joey' (coppery orange, paler at the edges), 'Piccadilly' (scarlet, pale yellow reverse), 'Pink Favourite' (deep pink) and 'Wendy Cussons' (deep reddish pink).

Similarly, the floribunda (cluster-flowered bush) roses have much to offer: 'Anne Harkness' (apricot pink), 'Arthur Bell' (golden yellow), 'City of Leeds' (rich salmon pink), 'Dame of Sark' (golden yellow, flushed scarlet). 'Evelyn Fison' (vivid scarlet), 'Iceberg' (white), 'Mountbatten' (mimosa yellow) and 'Southampton' (apricot orange, flushed scarlet).

When we come to consider shrub or species roses for autumn colour there are few flowerers; the China rose 'Old Blush' is an exception (it will flower into the winter). The majority are more often grown for their large and extremely decorative autumn hips. Included here are *Rosa moyesii* 'Geranium' with a height and spread of around 2.1 m (7 ft). The long glossy red hips last well into winter.

Then there is *R. rubrifolia* with a height of 2.1 m (7 ft), and a spread of 1.5 m (5 ft). Bunches of bright red hips follow the deep pink summer flowers. *R. rugosa* has a number of worthwhile varieties, notably those which provide flowers at the same time as the hips. These include 'Frau Dagmar Hartopp' (shell pink blooms with superb red hips) and 'Scabrosa' (mauve blooms and large tomato-like hips).

SKIMMIA

A neat, compact shrub which produces tiny scented white flowers in spring. Male plants flower more freely, but the females produce the attractive autumn berries. Plants of both sexes will be required if the berries are desired. These shrubs prefer sandy or peaty soils, and dislike chalk.

S. japonica. Aromatic, leathery evergreen leaves are produced on this shrub 90–150 cm (3–5 ft) high, with a spread of 1.5–1.8 m (5–6 ft). Clusters of brilliant red berries, the size of large peas, remain on bushes throughout winter and until spring.

STRANVAESIA

A small group of hardy evergreen shrubs, only one species of which is generally found in cultivation. A well-drained lime-free soil is appreciated, and as it is a little on the tender side, some form of nearby shelter would not go amiss.

S. davidiana. A vigorous shrub reaching an ultimate height and spread of 3.6–4.8 m (12–16 ft). Its leaves, berries and general habit resemble those of a large cotoneaster. Although classed as an evergreen, only the younger foliage will remain green over winter; the older leaves turn to scarlet before they fall. In addition, clusters of bright red berries – generally ignored by birds – cover the bush and last well into winter.

A sunny spot suits *Schizostylis coccinea* (Kaffir lily,
or crimson flag).

SYMPHORICARPOS
(SNOWBERRY)

A group of shrubs which produces suckers from the roots. These soon develop into a thicket and your one plant may soon become a dense border. Slender stems carry tiny blush-white summer flowers which are followed by the characteristic long-lasting white or pink berries. These thrive in nearly all soils and situations, even under trees.

S. albus. This species will reach a height of 1.5–2.1 m (5–7 ft). Its suckering habit will allow it to spread indefinitely. Snow white berries like marbles are produced, and these will persist almost until the spring.

S × doorenbosii. A smaller shrub, this will grow to about 1.5 m (5 ft) in height. Berries are white, tinged rose pink. The form 'Magic Berry' has an abundance of rose pink berries.

VIBURNUM

There are so many different types of viburnum that we could almost fill our gardens with them and not have two alike! They can be broadly divided into two categories: evergreen or deciduous. Well cultivated soils incorporating good quantities of organic matter to retain moisture are the ideal for all species. Many winter-flowering types have a delicious fragrance, while others carry richly coloured berries and bright autumn leaf tints. It has to be said, however, that those with some of the best autumn foliage are not really garden-worthy in any other respect; they are often found growing wild or in hedgerows, where they excel. The types which follow are mainly grown for their autumn fruits.

V. betulifolium. This deciduous species has a bushy habit and reaches up to 3.6 m (12 ft) in height and spread. It may be a few years before this species sets berry for the first time, but it will certainly be worth the wait. The fruits hang like redcurrants in large, spectacular clusters.

V. davidii. An evergreen shrub, somewhat smaller at around 90 cm (3 ft) in height, with a 1.5 m (5 ft) spread. It is suitable for ground cover purposes, and produces small turquoise blue berries if male and female plants are grown together.

V. opulus (guelder rose). Deciduous, and one of the largest of all viburnums with a height and spread of up to 4.5 m (15 ft). The dark green maple-like leaves turn a bright rosy crimson before falling. The late spring flowers are followed by translucent red autumn berries. The form 'Sterile' (snowball bush) has huge white flower clusters and velvety crimson-orange leaf tints. 'Xanthocarpum' is one of the best of all autumn fruiting shrubs, with rich yellow berries.

VITIS (ORNAMENTAL VINE)

Another of the climbers, and closely related to parthenocissus (Virginia creeper), this large genus includes the many forms of wine and dessert grapes. There are really only two species grown in gardens for their spectacular autumn leaves. All vines are suitable for growing on walls, over a pergola or trellis, or through old trees. Ordinary moisture-retentive soils, neither too acid nor too chalky, are ideal.

V. coignetiae (Japanese crimson glory vine). This will grow over a wall from its base to around 27 m (90 ft). It has huge, leathery leaves which change colour slowly at first, eventually erupting in a riot of intense orange-carmine colour, tinged with scarlet.

V. vinifera 'Brandt'. Here we have one of the wine grapes, growing to a height and spread of around 6 m (20 ft). Bunches of succulent sweet, aromatic grapes are produced if treated right, as well as the attractive crimson, pink and orange leaf tints.

CHAPTER FOUR

BORDER PLANTS IN AUTUMN

The first chapter of this book, on trees, included very few autumn-flowering subjects. The second chapter, on shrubs, discussed rather more, and this chapter deals exclusively with autumn floral offerings.

The herbaceous border is largely a thing of the past. A hundred years ago it was an essential feature of the larger garden; it was generally long and narrow, with either a wall or clipped hedge acting as a backcloth. In it were 'herbaceous perennials' which die down every winter and produce new stems and leaves each spring. The best way, obviously, to arrange the plants within the border was to have the tall-growing varieties at the back and set the clumps of low-growing plants at the front.

Nowadays it is much more common to see 'mixed' borders. Here we have a mix of herbaceous perennials, deciduous and evergreen shrubs, annuals and flowering bulbs. The rigid rules of the old perennial borders have been abandoned to allow temporary, short-lived plants to have equal prominence with the other plant occupants.

Border plants – or perennials in the context of this chapter – have an important part to play in our gardening scene. They are among the most diverse of plants in shape and colour. They range in height from 15–20cm (6–8in) for violets, to about 2.4m (8ft) with *Macleaya cordata* (plume poppy).

Of course, autumn is the season when those two hobby plants, chrysanthemums and dahlias, really come into their own. These do not fit into the context of this chapter happily – they are not exactly perennials, nor are they true border plants. Some forms, too, can be grown in pots in a greenhouse.

Beginners are often confused by the resemblance between these two garden giants. To the enthusiast, however, they are as different as chalk from cheese. But what exactly are the differences? At first glance it is hard to see. Both types of plant are related, although distantly, to the daisy, and both have been so bred over recent years that they can be in flower every month of the year and in nearly all the colours under the sun (except for true blue and black).

It is when you take a close look at each in turn that you can begin to see the dissimilarities. Let's start by examining the dahlia. The earliest to bloom start in high summer and continue until the first sharp autumn frosts: it is fairly common, in sheltered parts, to cut flower heads from the garden on bonfire night!

Once established, a dahlia quickly grows into a sturdy bush covered in blooms. Some large-flowered plants will produce more than 100 blooms in a season – provided they are given sufficient water and food. This is nothing, however, when compared to the pompons (or 'drumstick' types) which have small globular blooms with petals that fold inwards. These are capable of carrying 100 blooms in one flush! With colour in mind, some varieties have flowers that are one shade all over, while others may be tipped, spotted or striped with two or more colours.

The range of shades is almost matched by the range of shapes! We are, perhaps, more familiar with the round flowers of the broad-petalled decoratives and the pompons, but there are other dahlias resembling roses, asters, carnations, chrysanthemums (of course), and even orchids.

Few nurseries today seem to offer dahlia tubers by mail order, so more often than not you need to visit a large garden shop which sells them in packs. To sum up the dahlia – it's a dramatic garden plant that is easy to grow, and tolerant of a wide range of conditions. To the uninitiated, the most obvious difference between these and chrysanthemums is not the flower, but the foliage. Dahlias have glossy mid-green, serrated, fleshy leaves, whereas chrysanthemums are a deep green with rounded or lobed edges.

Now on to the chrysanthemums (or 'mums' as the commercial floristry trade calls them), which are surpassed only by the rose as our Number 1 garden plant for the enthusiast. Outwardly, mums are grown for much the same reason as dahlias: to brighten the garden with large splashes of vivid colours, to cut for decoration indoors and, with the really keen grower, to cultivate perfect blooms for exhibiting at local, county and national shows.

The florist's mums are divided into two groups: early-flowering (outdoor) and late-flowering (indoor), according to their natural flowering time. They are further classified under similar descriptive group headings as dahlias (although pompon is really the only category actually shared by both plants). Incurved, reflexed, intermediate, spider and spoon-shaped are all descriptions of how chrysanthemum petals lie.

The growing techniques and cultivation of mums are not the same as for dahlias. Mums do not have tubers; shops and nurseries sell them usually as rooted cuttings. A choice plant will have healthy, rich green leaves, be sturdy and short jointed. Mail order cuttings can be dispatched in the depths of winter for growing on throughout spring before planting outdoors, but you will need a heated greenhouse to look after them well.

It is common practice to arrange a bed or border to produce colour from the dawn of spring to the last throes of autumn, and if plants are chosen carefully this is quite possible, even in the smallest of borders. Sometimes borders are planned to be at their best during one season only, and these invariably look spectacular when in full bloom. Where there is sufficient room, it is an excellent idea to have a border of this kind, provided it doesn't dominate the garden. If autumn is your chosen season, any of the following border perennials would not disappoint you. In a small garden, however, it would be a better idea to spread the colour and interest over as long a period as possible.

ACONITUM (MONKSHOOD)

This easy-to-grow group of plants is ideal if your garden has more than its fair share of shade from either buildings or nearby trees. Their main requirement is a soil rich in organic matter. The leaves are deeply cut, and the helmeted blue flowers show an obvious relationship to the common border delphiniums. It should be noted that, despite their beauty, all parts of these plants are poisonous.

A. carmichaelii (syn. *A. fischeri*). A height of 90cm (3ft) can be expected. They should not be planted closer than 45cm (1½ft) apart. The stems are clothed with dark green leaves and violet-blue flowers from late summer onwards.

ANEMONE (JAPANESE ANEMONE)

These must not be confused with the low-growing spring-flowering forms. The anemone genus is a large and diverse one. The spring bloomers are more suited to rock garden or pot culture, while the summer and autumn flowering border types discussed here are fibrous-rooted, long-lived and trouble-free if grown in well-drained soil. Poppy-flowered types, which are tuberous-rooted, are covered on p.57. Saucer-

So loved by bees and butterflies: the rusty brown flowers of *Sedum spectabile* 'Autumn Joy'.

shaped flowers and deeply lobed leaves are the characteristics of the Japánese anemones. Sometimes they can take a year or two before offering their first flowers. Also they have been known to suffer in harsh winters, so leave the old and dead flower stems on the plants until spring – these will afford some weather protection.

A. japonica (syn. *A. hybrida*). Extremely easy-to-grow plants, with a spreading but not invasive habit. They will reach a height of around 60–90cm (2–3ft), with a planting distance of about 45cm (1½ft). The variety 'September Charm' has soft pink single flowers with golden yellow centres. 'Queen Charlotte' is the same colour, but has a fuller, semi-double bloom. 'White Queen' is a pure white-flowered, strong-growing form.

ASTER

Although there are some annual and shrubby asters, we mainly see the herbaceous kinds, including Michaelmas daisies, planted in our gardens. They need little introduction, for the great progress made during the last 40 years or so in raising a large number of new varieties has firmly established them among the most popular and useful border perennials. Part of the criteria of this research has been the introduction of later-flowering varieties, and now we have them blooming until the first frosts. Colours range through white, pink, red, blue, mauve and purple, many with double flowers. They grow well in most kinds of soil, but prefer a sunny situation.

A. amellus. This species is not seen as often as it should, mainly due to its being slower growing than other asters. Soft grey-green foliage is topped by white single daisy-like flowerheads. Growing to a height of around 60cm (2ft), they should be set about 45cm (1½ft) apart. The form 'King George' is light lavender blue, while 'Nocturne' is rosy mauve.

A. × frikartii. This is a hybrid between *A. amellus* and *A. thompsonii*, and is a welcome addition. Light lavender blue flowers appear on branching stems. A height of 90cm (3ft) can be expected, and they should be set 60cm (2ft) apart.

A. novi-belgii (Michaelmas daisy). The largest and most popular group of asters. All have a dense, bushy habit with rather woody stems. This species has an extremely wide range of heights, the dwarfer kinds receiving prominence in recent years. These include 'Dandy', purple-red, 30cm (1ft); 'Jenny', violet purple, 30cm (1ft); and 'Little Pink Beauty', pink, semi-double blooms, 40cm (16in). Slightly taller are 'Carnival', cherry red, semi-double, 60cm (2ft); 'Freda Ballard', rich red, semi-double, 90cm (3ft); and 'Marie Ballard', light blue, double, 90cm (3ft).

CENTRANTHUS (VALERIAN)

A small group of Mediterranean plants particularly suitable for dry conditions such as are found in rock gardens and walls, but also perfectly happy in the moister soils of beds and borders. A fully sunny spot is the best position. An introduced plant in a favoured situation will soon set seed, and 'wild' forms may spring up all over the place.

C. ruber 'Coccineus'. This is the only form worthy of garden space. Scarlet flowers appear on stems 45–90cm (1½–3ft) tall. The planting distance should be 30cm (1ft); this way a number of plants together will give a big, bold splash.

CIMICIFUGA (BUGBANE)

These are familiar woodland plants, generally with white, plume-like flowering spikes in late summer and autumn. Any kind of soil will do, and part or dense shade will be tolerated.

C. foetida. Although a height of 1.2–1.5m

(4–5ft) can be reached, the plants are very upright, and planting them only 60cm (2ft) apart is not too close. The form 'White Pearl' is more commonly available, but the later-flowering 'Elstead Variety' is well worth seeking out.

CORTADERIA (PAMPAS GRASS)

Familiar to almost everyone, the pampas grass throws up those magnificent, long silky feathery plumes every summer. These are extremely hardy and are suitable for inclusion in herbaceous, shrub or mixed borders, or simply as specimen plants on their own. A sunny position in a well-drained soil is all that is desired. The plumes are useful for indoor decoration, but they should really be cut as young as possible. They should then be sun-dried for two or three days, and then left in a shed until the stems are completely dry.

C. selloana **'Sunningdale Silver'.** The best of the varieties generally available. Although the plumes appear in summer, they stay on the plant and look as fresh as ever until late autumn. They will eventually fall and by spring, when the plants should be tidied up, they will have disintegrated. The height of these plumes may reach a staggering 2.1–3m (7–10ft). Planting distance: at least 1.8m (6ft).

ECHINACEA (PURPLE CONEFLOWER)

This is an offshoot from the closely related yellow-flowered rudbeckia (coneflower). Echinaceas have brilliant warm shades of red-purple. Although not particularly fussy, they tend to do better in good, loamy soils and a sunny position.

E. purpurea. It will attain a maximum height of 1.2m (4ft) in your border; planting distance is 45–60cm (1½–2ft). The cone-shaped purple-crimson blooms have orange centres. Probably the best form is 'Robert Bloom' (purple-rose) with blooms hanging fast until mid-autumn.

LIRIOPE

Not often seen, this long-lived plant will grow particularly well in lime-free soil. It will tolerate quite heavy shade, as well as prolonged hot sun. Originally from the Far East, this little beauty is ideal for the front of your border.

L. muscari (syn. *L. platyphylla).* The only species worth garden space. Clumps of broad grassy leaves are pierced by 30cm (12in) high spikes of violet-mauve pokers. It's a bright and charming plant, lasting almost into winter. Planting distance: 40cm (15in).

PHLOX

These beautiful red/mauve/white border plants make a terrific contribution towards colourful gardens in late summer and autumn, when yellows and oranges generally predominate. There is a vast number of varieties now in existence. They prefer good, light soil and are least happy on chalky clay though, even here, they will respond well to a little peat and sand incorporated into the soil. The major problem faced by phlox growers is that of the possibility of eelworm infestation. This little pest invades the stems and shoots, but the roots are left alone, so taking root cuttings is the most efficient method of propagation (as well as sowing seed). (See also p120.) Most of our familiar and respected border phloxes have been derived from one species.

P. paniculata (syn. *P. decussata).* A height of 1.2m (4ft) may be attained – depending on variety. Planting distance: 45–60cm (1½-2ft). The mid-green leaves are obscured, from high summer, by richly coloured flowers. The following four varieties are particularly good: 'Balmoral', bold heads of light, clear pink; 'Brigadier', glowing scarlet salmon; 'Starfire', deep red; and 'White Diamond', the purest of whites.

PHYSALIS (CHINESE LANTERN, BLADDER CHERRY)

During high summer this plant is not at all spectacular – leafy, bushy growth and insignificant white flowers. But once the leaves begin to fall in autumn, then the fascinating orange bags, each containing a small similarly coloured fruit, are revealed. These pods are ideal for use by flower arrangers. The plants seem to grow well in any well-drained soil.

P. alkekengii franchetii. The most commonly available form, with a height and planting distance of 60cm (2ft). The vivid orange bladders or 'lanterns' hang on the plants well into winter.

PHYSOSTEGIA (OBEDIENT PLANT)

An easy plant to grow, its individual tubular flowers have the curious ability to stay in place when moved away from their natural position – hence the common name. A little water in dry weather and a medium to good soil is all that this tallish perennial demands.

P. virginiana 'Vivid'. This is the form with most autumn appeal. Deep pink flowers are carried on stems up to 75cm (2½ft) – sometimes more – in height. Set these plants 60cm (2ft) apart.

RUDBECKIA (CONEFLOWER)

A popular plant, often grown specially for its autumn floral offerings, although it starts its show in mid-summer. Gold, orange and yellow (and combinations of the three) are the colours in question, and it is worth knowing that the cut blooms last a long while in water. A sunny or lightly shaded spot is best, in any reasonable garden soil.

R. fulgida (syn. *R. deamii*). Deep, butter yellow, star-shaped flowers with black cen-tres are massed over mid-green leaves. Height: 60–90cm (2–3ft). Planting distance: 60cm (2ft).

R. 'Goldsturm'. This has blooms of a deeper yellow, and they will last until late autumn. Height and planting distance: 60cm (2ft).

SAXIFRAGA (SAXIFRAGE)

This is an extremely large and varied group of plants, with nearly 400 types from which to choose. Most are grown in small borders, rockeries, or in containers in an unheated greenhouse. Very few are autumn flowerers, and only one is recommended for this purpose.

S. fortunei. White flowers are thought by some to be a waste of colour! But when, with careful planning, you have a riot of colour in autumn, a little white here and there is a cool, welcome relief, specially when the flowers are delicate and lacy, as with this autumn-flowering saxifrage. Any soil or situation will suit this particular form, as long as it is not consistently wet through inadequate drainage. Height: 45cm (1½ft). Planting distance: 60cm (2ft).

SCABIOSA (SCABIOUS, PINCUSHION FLOWER)

Our countryside meadows and fields frequently throw forth wild scabious, providing dots of blue against the backgrounds of wheat or barley. There are a number of worthwhile garden forms, with new introductions over recent years. An open, sunny site is preferred, and any reasonable soil will do.

S. caucasica. The best known of all, with mid-green leaves and lavender blue flowers on stems 60cm (2ft) high. Set plants about 45cm (1½ft) apart. Three forms are worth mentioning: 'Bressingham White', pure white; 'Butterfly Blue', violet-blue; and 'Clive Greaves', rich mauve. All will provide blooms through till mid-autumn.

One of the many types of autumn-flowering colchicum,
C.speciosum produces mauve blooms 15cm (6in) high.

SCHIZOSTYLIS (KAFFIR LILY, CRIMSON FLAG)

This fascinating perennial will add good colour to your border from the beginning of autumn onwards. Accompanying the grass-like foliage are tall flowering spikes which are topped by wide open crocus-like blooms. Unfortunately schizostylis do not always come through hard, prolonged winters but they are generally fine in milder areas. A sunny spot is best, in well-drained, light soil. They grow well, too, in pots in an unheated greenhouse.

S. coccinea. Originally from South Africa, this species will provide you with scarlet blooms on 90cm (3ft) stems. Planting distance: 30cm (1ft). A couple of notable varieties are 'Major', deep red, and 'Viscountess Byng', pink (blooms do not open until mid-autumn).

SEDUM (STONECROP)

A group of over 600 species, covering a wide range of colours, shapes, habits, and requirements. For the purposes of this book, we will concentrate on just one species.

S. spectabile. Broad, fleshy white-green leaves are carried on stems up to 60cm (2ft) high. Plant this species 45cm (1½ft) apart. Fluffy flower heads often as wide as your hand are particularly attractive to bees and butterflies. Most bloom well into autumn, and the following varieties are worth trying: 'Carmen', rose red; 'Meteor', carmine red; and 'Autumn Joy', salmon pink turning rusty brown.

STOKESIA (STOKES' ASTER)

Very showy flowers, which are good for cutting and indoor decoration, are provided by this hardy perennial. A light and free-draining soil is preferred, and any situation except dense shade. The blooms appear first in mid-summer and continue until the first frosts of autumn.

S. laevis (syn. *S. cyanea*). Long, narrow mid-green leaves accompany the saucer-shaped, deeply notched pale mauve flowers. This species will reach a height of 45cm (18in), and should be planted at a distance of 40–45cm (15–18in). The form 'Blue Star' has light blue blooms up to 8cm (3in) across, and is one of the best. Prolong the flowering season by removing the faded blooms on a regular basis.

VIOLA (SWEET VIOLET)

Although the genus covers over 500 species, including pansies, only one species is of interest to us here. Most soil types are suitable, but heavy soils are made more acceptable by the addition of well-decayed compost. On hot, dry soils a semi-shaded site is desirable, otherwise they will thrive best in an open, sunny position.

V. odorata. The year's main flush of flowers occurs from late winter to early spring, but very often a secondary flush will delight us in autumn. The heart-shaped leaves are mid to dark green, while the delicate flowers come in shades of purple or white. The plants reach no higher than 15–20cm (6–8in), and they should be planted around 23cm (9in) apart.

CHAPTER FIVE

BULBS IN AUTUMN

Keeping the garden colourful and exciting after the summer flowers fade away can be a bit of a problem if there isn't much room to spare for late-flowering perennial border plants, or for the masses of trees and shrubs grown for their autumn berries and leaf tints. However, and with a few exceptions, autumn-flowering bulbs can be easily and quickly popped into the ground for an almost immediate effect, without taking up a lot of valuable space.

There is something about a bulb itself which makes it attractive even in its dry, unplanted state. It is interesting to look at, smooth to handle, bulging and full of promise of pleasure in store. Add to this the fact that most bulbs can be taken out of the soil for a period of time, and kept dry, which makes them easier to market and sell (if you are a supplier), and ideal for a temporary garden situation (if, as a gardener, you crave change).

It is perhaps during spring when we get most pleasure from bulbs in the garden. Daffodils, tulips, crocuses and hyacinths light up our plots with much needed colour after two or three relatively drab months. But the other seasons are not devoid of bulb plantlife. Summer probably has more to offer us in the way of bulbs, but we are perhaps not as familiar with the offerings. Winter has a few excellent subjects (see pp.91–96), and autumn has a dozen or so attractive forms which enhance this (as we have already discovered) colourful season.

Whereas the majority of spring-flowering bulbs are planted in beds and borders to provide us with large groups and 'drifts' of colour, the autumn-flowering types are rather more delicate in appearance and are really seen at their best in groups of two or three, or naturalized in lawn or wooded areas. Other suitable planting sites are among shrubs, under large spreading trees or planted in a rock garden. The latter situation is ideal for the smaller subjects like *Crocus speciosum* (autumn crocus), *Cyclamen hederifolium* (syn. *C. neapolitanum*) and *Sternbergia lutea* (yellow star flower).

Autumn-flowering bulbs should be ordered early from catalogues, to go into the ground in mid-summer; late planted bulbs will often have started sprouting and may subsequently produce a poor display. But one thing is for sure, a few of these subjects in the garden will certainly make winter seem less long!

ACIDANTHERA

Apart from the virtue of flowering in autumn, this bulb has very attractive, highly fragrant blooms. Any well-drained soil will suit this beauty. One word of warning though; acidantheras come from tropical Africa and are tender in cooler zones. This means that the corms must be lifted before winter sets in. These should then be stored in a warm dry place before planting time again, in late spring. In cold, exposed areas they are, perhaps, best grown in pots in the greenhouse. Although there are quite a few species, only one form is generally available.

A. bicolor murielae. The starry flowers and sword-shaped leaves give this form a gladiolus-like appearance (they are related, distantly). The 5cm (2in) wide blooms,

An outdoor cyclamen particularly recommended for its autumn blooms is the 8–15 cm (3–6 in) high *C. hederifolium*.

which first appear in mid-summer, bear white petals, each with a distinct purple base. A height of 90cm (3ft) can be achieved. Space plants about 23cm (9in) apart.

AMARYLLIS (BELLADONNA LILY)

Another half-hardy subject, the best place to grow this is in a dry border next to a sunny south-facing wall. Given a good place like this, it will reward you with a display of large, colourful flowers lasting two months or more. The blooms are recommended for cutting and indoor decoration.

A. belladonna. The strap-shaped mid-green leaves appear in spring and die down in early summer. About six weeks later the thick flower stalk appears, topped by a cluster of three or four fragrant pink or salmon blooms. These flowers are about 8cm (3in) across, and each has a yellow throat. The 60cm (2ft) high flower stalks need staking if they are to avoid wind damage. Space plants 30cm (1ft) apart.

ANEMONE (WINDFLOWER)

We have already looked at the perennial Japanese anemones (p.48), and to show just how diverse this large genus is, the tuberous-rooted types discussed here bear hardly any resemblance. These poppy-flowered kinds are very popular, and appreciate a well-drained humus-rich soil in sun or light shade. The flowering period depends on the planting time. Planting in late autumn will give flowers in late winter (but some protection, such as that given by a cloche, will be required), while planting in mid-spring will give flowers from the beginning of autumn. It should be noted that plants deteriorate after two years, so replacing with fresh plants is the only real alternative.

A. coronaria. Height: 15–30cm (6–12in). Planting distance: 10–15cm (4–6in). This is the species, descended from which are the two most popular strains of florists' poppy-flowered anemones: the De Caen types produce single blooms in a dazzling mixture of red, white and blue – one plant may produce 20 blooms. St Brigid, meanwhile, is a double or semi-double strain with similar colours to those of De Caen, but with fewer blooms to each plant.

COLCHICUM (AUTUMN CROCUS)

Despite the shape of the flowers – and the common name – this group of plants is not, in fact, related to the crocus at all. Over the years it has had a succession of common names, including naked ladies and naked boys, but that of autumn crocus seems to have stayed, not least because colchicums do resemble crocuses. In autumn the wineglass-shaped blooms poke through the soil. These flowers die when winter frosts arrive, and then in spring the large, cabbage-like leaves furnish the ground with untidy greenery. Any reasonably fertile well-drained soil will do, as will a sunny or lightly shaded spot.

C. autumnale. The lilac coloured flowers (several per corm) reach a height of around 15cm (6in). The spring leaves may reach 25cm (10in). Space plants 23cm (9in) apart. The form 'Album' produces pure white blooms, while 'Roseum Plenum' is a double rose pink variety.

C. speciosum. Mauve 15cm (6in) tall autumn blooms are followed by spring leaves 40cm (16in) high. Space plants 23–30cm (9–12in) apart. The variety 'Lilac Wonder' is deep lilac pink with white stripes, 'Violet Queen' is deep mauve with a thin white stripe on each petal, and 'Waterlily' has large double mauve blooms.

CROCOSMIA (MONTBRETIA)

A small group of plants with attractive, vividly coloured blooms. Grown from a corm, this plant likes to have its feet in a well-drained soil in a sunny position. In less temperate gardens some winter protection would be appreciated. The flowers, when cut, last well in water.

C. × crocosmiiflora. This produces a spreading clump of sword-like mid-green leaves. Bright orange trumpet-shaped flowers in zig-zag fashion clothe the stems from late summer onwards. The form 'Vulcan' is very bright, with burnt orange-red blooms. Height: 60–90cm (2–3ft). Set plants 10–15cm (4–6in) apart.

CROCUS

This group of plants hardly needs an introduction. Most of the species flower in the spring, but a few do so in autumn and winter. All grow in most garden soils in sun or shade and are also suitable for rock gardens. Whereas the spring-flowering varieties can be seen in pale blue, purple, white, cream, yellow and bronze (plus striped and bicoloured forms), the autumn types are limited to white, lilac or purple. One of the true autumn crocuses, C. sativus (saffron crocus), is attractive with its lilac, red-centred flowers, but is extremely difficult to grow outdoors as it requires a long, hot summer to ripen its corms.

C. speciosus. This is the most popular of the true autumn crocuses, perhaps because it is easy to grow. Its lilac-blue blooms stand 10–13 (4–5in) high. 'Albus' is the pure white form, and 'Oxonian' is purple.

CYCLAMEN

Unlikely as it may seem, this is a distant relation of the primrose. For many of us the cyclamen is a winter greenhouse or pot plant bearing large, long-stemmed pink or white flowers with swept-back petals. But there are a number of smaller forms which enjoy a cool, shady spot outdoors. As far as soil goes, a well-drained, humus-rich one is preferred.

Careful selection of species could enable you to have hardy cyclamen blooming right through the year. There is, however, one form particularly recommended for its autumn blooms.

C. hederifolium (syn. C. neapolitanum). This produces stunning white or pink flowers from early autumn, and then makes a handsome carpet of silver-patterned leaves from autumn to late spring. The flowers stand 8–15cm (3–6in) high, and the tubers should be set about 15cm (6in) apart.

GALANTHUS (SNOWDROP)

Another small bulbous plant that needs no introduction. Any moist soil will do, and a partly shaded spot is preferred. The winter blooms are generally the first to light up the garden. There are, however, a couple of uncommon autumn-flowering snowdrops which bloom before the leaves appear. Only one is worthy of space here.

G. nivalis reginae-olgae. An uncommon form and a little expensive to buy, but generally stocked by the large bulb houses, and not just for the snowdrop enthusiast. The white petals with central green blotches are carried on 15cm (6in) high stems during mid-autumn. Plant bulbs 10–15cm (4–6in) apart.

NERINE

This group of plants is generally considered to be too tender to grow outdoors – they originally came from South Africa. But there is one form which never fails to flower outside. Clusters of large, open, long-lasting blooms are held high on leafless stalks. A well-drained soil and full sun are essential.

N. bowdenii. Deep pink blooms are held on stems 45cm (1½ft) high. The strap-shaped leaves are 30cm (1ft) long and give the plant a stately, arching habit. Set plants around 15cm (6in) apart.

A well-drained soil and full sun are essential for pink-flowered
Nerine bowdenii.

STERNBERGIA (YELLOW STAR FLOWER)

This is a native of the Middle East (often reputed to be the plant in mind when Jesus referred to 'the lilies of the field'). At first glance this autumn beauty looks like a golden yellow crocus. But a closer look will indicate that sternbergia blooms are borne on individual stems, whereas crocus flowers are, botanically, an extension of a petal tube.

Ideal for rockeries and other free-draining areas, this plant is notoriously slow to establish. A chalky soil is preferred. One thing – sternbergias hate being disturbed. Lifting and replanting will invariably end in death!

S. lutea. This is the only species commonly found. The shining yellow blooms are carried about 10cm (4in) from the soil, and plants should be set 10–15cm (4–6in) apart. The form 'Angustifolia' is generally more free with its blooms.

PART 2
WINTER

CHAPTER SIX

WINTER COLOUR

I asked a non-gardener, 'What is the best thing about winter?' 'Sitting in front of a warm fire,' he replied. Ask a keen gardener the same question, and the answer could well be: 'Cornus bark', or 'Witch hazels in flower', or 'A huge patch of snowdrops'. For winter really does have a beauty of its own. The same colours are available to us as in summer, except they are carried on fewer types of plant. The blooms which appear during our colder months can compare in brilliance with the more obvious beauty that the summer's sun brings out. Certainly winter blooms have a charm, and may be even more appreciated on account of their scarcity.

As far as general gardening is concerned, there really is nothing to do in the way of routine maintenance, but sit back (possibly in front of that warm fire), and view the garden from a distance. This doesn't suggest a dereliction of duty, however, because in many instances it can do more harm than good to traipse around the garden during the depths of winter. After all, the ground cannot and should not be dug when it is frosty or snow-covered, nor should the lawn be walked upon (it will cause brown patches after the thaw), and it's too cold to take cuttings or sow seeds. So my recommendation for winter gardening is: keep to the shed or greenhouse, and catch up with work in those quarters. Alternatively, sit back and watch the results of your handiwork.

When does winter start and finish? There can be no hard and fast distinction. In my view we are into winter when the true deciduous trees and shrubs have dropped their last leaves, and the average outdoor temperature is sufficient to send a chill through one's outer clothing, even though one might be wrapped up well! The winter quarter comes to an end around Easter, but don't forget that snow can fall heavily in Britain during late spring. In reality then, I regard winter to last for a period of about four months.

In one category, at least, winter scores over autumn. There are four types of colour that can be had in the winter garden – one more than those in the previous season. As with autumn, our coldest season has its own proliferation of leaves (including evergreens), flowers and berries. But there is also the new attraction of colourful and interesting bark or twigs. Perhaps the most striking difference between winter and the other seasons is the lack of foliage on deciduous plants. Only when the leaves fall do the open heads of trees and shrubs become apparent, and the reds and golds of cornus branches, and the stark white of rubus, lend their beauty to the scene. Consider, too, the stately *Fraxinus excelsior* (common ash), which has a graceful open head and thick knobbly twigs tipped by black felted buds. Dare I say it's almost as attractive naked as when in leaf?

Flowerwise, there are rather more around at this time of year than in autumn. We can actually regard autumn as being the end of the growing year, and – although winter is really a dormant period in our climate – it can in some instances be looked upon as the beginning of the next.

It is a sure sign that spring is on the way when you begin to notice the male catkins on the hazel bushes in hedgerows and coppices. The little female blooms are less conspicuous, but if you look carefully you will find them scattered along the twigs, often quite

A lovely winter feature of the slow-growing *Acer griseum*
(paper bark maple).

close to the catkins. Other catkin-bearing trees and shrubs indicate, too, that winter is anything but a 'dead' time of year.

Take flowering bulbs for example: there are practically twice the number producing colour in the depths of winter as there are in mid-autumn. Similar can be said of garden shrubs, although these we are now considering more for their flowers and not at all for leaf tints.

And on the subject of leaves, there is little doubt that were the development of foliage given the same care and study that we bestow on flowers, our gardens would be very much more interesting. With many trees and shrubs the foliage is of paramount importance – it lasts for up to twelve months of the year, whereas the flowers are over in maybe two or three weeks. In winter, persistent foliage comes into its own: consider the golds and blues of conifers, the rich greenery of evergreen shrubs and the lingering crispy brown of the beech hedges. We must not forget, too, the variety of foliage we can now command in the garden. There is an almost infinite number of shapes and variety of colours: greys, greens, yellows, blues, and purples and variegated types.

The last main area of winter colour is that of fruits and berries. Where does this differ from autumn?, I hear you ask. The fruit-bearing plants so far discussed in this book were chosen because their peak of glory came

firmly within the autumn period. Many of these berried treasures will have lost their main colour – either through natural shedding, spoiling by frost, or as a result of bird interference. Now we shall be looking at those subjects which are somewhat later in their fruit production. Although they are fewer than in autumn, we can still rely on several to give us bright colour through the short, cold days of winter.

When it comes to planning your garden with winter plants in mind, remember that they should be given a place where they are protected as much as possible from strong winds. Also, with winter being a cold and generally inhospitable season, it would be nice to have the facility of viewing the plants from the comfort of the house.

Several shrubs, such as *Chimonanthus praecox* (winter sweet), *Daphne mezereum* (mezereon) and *Viburnum farreri* (syn. *V. fragrans*), have such a delicious scent when in flower that it would be a great shame to miss this by siting them far from the house, or away from a path. Interestingly, these highly scented shrubs make up for the fact that the flowers are somewhat less than dramatic in appearance. So, in order to take full advantage of their latent beauty, careful attention should be given to their placing and, if possible, they should be given a solid background, in the form of a wall, fence or backcloth of evergreens.

CHAPTER SEVEN

TREES IN WINTER

And now, back to the subject of trees, except that this time we are looking at those types with winter appeal. Evergreen broad-leaved types are of particular interest in winter, and many have interestingly coloured or variegated leaves. All are least satisfactory, however, in towns where air pollution takes away the shine of their foliage, but this cannot be avoided, generally. After all, it is far better to inject some life into our industrial areas than to have them devoid and barren of tree-life.

All that has so far been said regarding the importance of trees in our gardens remains. At this time of the year we are also treated to the often surprising delights of naked bark and bare twigs. There are many beautiful trees which enhance the garden by offering decorative polished or flaking bark. Add to these the several species which dare to flower, as well as the few conifers with attractive winter foliage, and we have the ingredients for another chapter!

ACER (MAPLE)

We have twice already looked at acers. This time the genus is being included specifically for its beauty of bark. As a reminder, all of the maples are easy to grow. They are hardy, and sharp frosts do not worry them. When planting, it is best to add some soil enricher, such as peat, chopped bark, leaf-mould or compost.

A. capillipes. Originally from Japan, this form will reach a height and spread of around 9m (30ft). The young shoots have a reddish tinge to them. The green winter bark is striped white, lengthwise.

A. davidii (Father David's maple). This Chinese form has grey bark, striped white, especially if it is grown in a partially shaded spot. Height: 6m (20ft). Spread: 3m (10ft).

A. griseum (paper bark maple). A slow-growing tree that will eventually reach a height of 6m (20ft), with a spread of 3.6m (12ft). Orange and pale greeny-brown bark flakes off in large papery tatters to reveal lovely smooth cinnamon red patches underneath.

A. grosseri hersii. Another Chinese maple, this will grow to 7.5m (25ft) in height, with a spread of 4.5m (15ft). The greenish bark has dramatic white streaks.

A. palmatum 'Senkaki' (coral bark maple). Distinctive glossy coral bark on young shoots brightens the winter garden. Quite a rapid grower, it will reach 4.5m (15ft), with a spread of 2.4m (8ft).

A. pennsylvanicum (snakebark maple, moosewood). Its first common name comes from its obvious resemblance to a snake's skin: striped white and silver bark on a background of jade green. Height: 6m (20ft). Spread: 3m (10ft).

ALNUS (ALDER)

A small group of catkin-bearing trees which are seldom cultivated in gardens, mainly because some forms are so commonly seen growing in the wild, that little enthusiasm can be raised to introduce any into garden schemes. However, there are a couple of types which are particularly interesting in winter. They thrive in moist situations, and can be very attractive by the waterside. These are useful trees if you desire a fast-growing screen or hedge – but they are not suitable for chalky soils.

A. glutinosa (common alder). Only to be recommended for the larger garden, as it may reach a height of 12m (40ft), with a spread of 7.5m (25ft). But if you can accommodate it, interest will be created by the sticky young buds, followed by yellow catkins in late winter.

A. incana (grey alder). This is a very hardy tree, and useful for planting in cold, wet places. The dimensions are more or less the same as the common alder. It is the form 'Aurea' (golden speckled alder) which is of particular interest in winter. Yellowish coral pink catkins are carried on twigs of the same colour. The main branches and stems, however, are a warm orange-buff.

ARBUTUS (STRAWBERRY TREE)

Although the few species in this genus are evergreen – they possess dark green, leathery, toothed leaves – they have impressive peeling bark which can be enjoyed at any time of year. The arbutus is tolerant of most soils, even chalk (which is surprising as it is related to the lime-hating rhododendron). If possible, choose a warm, sunny and sheltered spot.

A. × andrachnoides (syn. A × hybrida). The chief attraction of this eventually wide-spreading tree is the superb cinnamon red peeling bark. The white flowers of late autumn and winter are followed by small red strawberry-like fruits. Height: 3m (10ft). Spread: 2.4m (8ft).

A. unedo. An altogether bigger subject, with a height of up to 6m (20ft), and a spread of around 3m (10ft). Dark evergreen leaves frame the gnarled limbs and rough shredding brown bark. White bell-shaped flowers are accompanied by red fruits which have remained from the previous year. The word *unedo* comes from the Latin *unus* (one) and *edo* (to eat), meaning 'to eat one only' – pleasant to consume, but in small doses!

AZARA

A small group of trees and shrubs with attractive evergreen leaves and fragrant flowers, originally from Chile. There is one form worthy of garden space: cultivate it in any ordinary fertile soil, preferably in a sheltered spot or near to a wall.

A. microphylla. The hardiest form, with heavily vanilla-scented yellow flowers opening in mid-winter. Although the blooms are minute, in ideal conditions they completely smother the branches. Small leaves and a frond-like arrangement of the branches give this small tree a most elegant appearance. Height: 6m (20ft). Spread 3.6–4.5m (12–15ft).

BETULA (BIRCH)

The birch is a familiar tree, mainly native to Britain and Europe. The main ornamental attributes of the group are the graceful elegant habit and silvery trunks. The rich yellow autumn leaf tints are a welcome bonus, making it one of our favourite specimen trees. The birches thrive on the poorest of soils, although the drier, shallower and chalkier types tend to slow down the rate of tree growth. Open, sunny positions are best.

B. costata. One of the best birches, but too rarely seen. Originally from the Far East, it has a creamy white often yellow-tinged bark which peels prettily in large flaky patches. Not for really small gardens, its height may reach 10.5m (35ft), with a spread of 6m (20ft).

B. nigra (river birch, red birch). This is notable for its chocolate brown shaggy bark which peels in strips to reveal a smooth creamy pink young underbark. It is often seen as a picturesque multi-stemmed tree, with a height and spread of around 7.5m (25ft). As its first common name suggests, this species is particularly at home on the banks of a stream or in a moist woodland

The round fruits, ripening to red, of *Arbutus unedo* (strawberry tree).

garden though it will not tolerate permanently waterlogged soil.

B. papyrifera (paper birch, canoe birch). This North American species is famous for its striking white outer bark, peeling from the trunk in thin papery layers. It is one of the largest birches, reaching an overall height of around 18m (60ft), with a spread of about 7.5m (25ft).

B. pendula (silver birch). The most familiar species, and very fast-growing. Its white bark and often drooping branches make it an excellent choice as a specimen tree in a large lawn. In mature trees the bark becomes rough, cracked and gnarled at the base, but this is not a demerit. Height: 9m (30ft). Spread 4.5m (15ft).

CEDRUS (CEDAR)

There are few conifers which are able to steal their way into the pages of this book, but one form I welcome with open arms is a familiar tree in parks and large stately gardens. Young cedars are conical in outline, but a mature specimen is a magnificent sight with its massive trunk supporting tiered branches. Plant in a well-drained soil that receives plenty of sun. As this genus provides year-round foliage and no flower colour, there must be a special reason for its inclusion here.

C. atlantica 'Glauca' (Blue Atlas cedar). This is widely grown specially for its blue-green needle foliage. Blue is a rare garden colour in winter, so any hint of it is welcome. Beware though: the height could reach 15m (50ft), with a spread of 7.5–9m (25–30ft).

CORYLUS (HAZEL)

On p.14 we spoke of the autumn spectacle of *C. avellana*. There is one form of this species which creates much interest after the leaves have fallen, and the nuts have been har-

vested. A sheltered, sunny position suits this beauty.

C. avellana 'Contorta' (corkscrew hazel). This is a slow-growing tree reaching a height of 2.4–3m (8–10ft), with a similar spread. In winter, when the shoots are bare, we are treated to the curiously twisted and twining shoots. They look almost as if a strong man has bent them as he would an iron rod. A good crop of catkins is produced in late winter.

MAGNOLIA

We have already looked at the autumn-flowering *M. grandiflora*, (see p.23). Now we consider a winter charmer. With this form a lime-free soil is preferred and, to protect the winter blooms, a site well sheltered from cold winds and the worst frosts is desirable. Unfortunately, once again, this is too big for the average modern garden, but if space permits, it is an unforgettable sight when in full bloom.

M. campbellii (pink tulip tree). This native of the Himalayas makes ultimately a height of 12–13.5m (40–45ft), with spreading branches reaching out as far as 9m (30ft). A certain disadvantage with this species is its reluctance to flower when young – it is often known for trees to be 20 years of age before flowers appear. The blooms themselves resemble huge deep purplish pink waterlilies, and appear first in mid-winter.

POPULUS (POPLAR)

Although this is a large and varied group of trees, they are all easy to grow. They are useful for planting in wet areas and wild forms are often found growing by rivers and streams. They are all fast growers with greedy, invasive roots which will soon work their way into building foundations or pipes if there is a hint of available moisture to be found. Consequently, it is good advice to plant them at least 25m (60ft) away from such objects. They are relatively unfussy when it comes to type of soil and situation. A sunny, open spot is preferred, and the following species is particularly fond of a chalk soil, where it will give attractive yellow and sometimes red autumn colour as a bonus.

P. × canescens. The winter appeal of this species is twofold. Mature specimens develop an attractive creamy grey trunk, and the male catkins in late winter are most decorative, being woolly and crimson up to 10cm (4in) long. It is a suckering tree, often forming thickets in much the same way as symphoricarpos (snowberry). Height: 9–12m (30–40ft). Spread: indefinite.

PRUNUS

We have already looked at three types of prunus for their autumnal beauty (pp.24–26), and the same opening remarks apply here. Here are four with winter appeal:

P. davidiana (Chinese peach). Despite the drawbacks of the dreaded peach leaf curl disease, to which this ornamental peach is prone, it is a superb choice for the winter garden. It provides attractive single pink blooms from mid-winter onwards. It will reach a height of around 6m (20ft), with a spread of 3.6–4.5m (12–15ft). The form 'Alba' bears dazzling white blooms. Flowers of both are seen to their best advantage if the trees are planted against a dark background.

P. 'Fudanzakura'. This round-headed tree will reach an ultimate height of around 4.5–6m (15–20ft), with a spread of 3–4.5m (10–15ft). Between late autumn and early spring the branches carry clusters of flowers 2.5–4cm (1–1½in) wide which are pink in bud, opening to white.

P. serrula. A native of China, this species is grown chiefly for its attractive winter bark, which peels in strips to reveal polished, red-brown new bark. The shine of the trunk is improved by constant rubbing with the hands – but this unlikely action is not essential! Height: 7.5m (25ft). Spread: 5.4m (18ft).

P. subhirtella 'Autumnalis' (autumn cherry). Small, semi-double, pale blush blooms first appear in late autumn and continue until mid-spring. A few sprigs, if cut, will last reasonably well indoors. Height and spread: up to 9m (30ft). The form 'Autumnalis Rosea' has flowers of a deeper pink.

SALIX (WILLOW)

There are many types of willow (some 500 species), but many are too large for today's small garden. In addition, the larger kinds are as notorious as poplar when it comes to damaging buildings in their relentless search for water. However, a few tree forms are suited to our gardens and have much winter appeal. A moist soil in a sunny position is best.

S. daphnoides (violet willow). This will reach a height of 7.5m (25ft), and a spread of around 4.5m (15ft). The leafless winter shoots are purple-violet and are covered with a most attractive white bloom. Yellow male catkins show up before the leaves appear in late winter and early spring.

S. matsudana 'Tortuosa'. This is similar in appearance, at this time of year, to *Corylus avellana* 'Contorta' (corkscrew hazel). Twisted and contorted branches are carried on stems 6m (20ft) or so high (on mature specimens). A spread of 4.5m (15ft) can be expected.

THUJA (ARBOR-VITAE)

This is a small group of evergreen coniferous trees, originally from the Far East and North America. The foliage is composed of flat scales, closely clothing the shoots. The young 'leaves' are more spreading and pointed than the older or 'adult' ones. Various people claim the leaves give off the aroma of crushed pineapple, cooked apples, or fruit cake with almonds! These conifers are easily grown in any ordinary garden soil, but do best in a moist deep soil and in a sheltered position in full sun. The common name of 'arbor-vitae' is regularly found in books, but seldom used in practice.

T. occidentalis 'Rheingold'. This is a slow-growing tree with golden yellow juvenile and adult foliage, the brightness of which is best seen in the winter sunshine. It is a small form of *T. occidentalis* (white cedar – although it is in no way a relation of the true cedar), and will reach a height of 1.8m (6ft), with a spread of 1.2m (4ft). (Some have found that the foliage in winter turns to a coppery shade.)

T. plicata (Western red cedar). The reddish brown trunk with spongy bark is interesting in this, the straight form. Highly fragrant glossy green scale-like leaves are held on branches which could be as much as 21m (70ft) high with a spread of 6.7m (25ft). Much better for general garden purposes in winter is the form 'Stoneham Gold', with golden young foliage, retaining much of its yellow sheen into the winter months, specially if sited in a sunny position. Height: around 3m (10ft). Spread: 1.5–1.8m (5–6ft).

CHAPTER EIGHT

SHRUBS AND CLIMBERS IN WINTER

The biggest splash of winter colour comes from the many deciduous shrubs which bloom steadfastly against the threats of the elements. Flowers in nearly every colour (except blue) are available, enabling us to enjoy a really warming range of hues. And, of course, it's not just the flowers of these deciduous beauties that make us look forward to their winter features – many have glossy winter stems that make them every bit as beautiful as their flowering cousins. Take, for example, the red stems of *Salix alba* 'Chermesina' (scarlet willow). In their own right they are brilliant, but grow them adjacent to the white-stemmed *Rubus cockburnianus* (whitewashed bramble), or the yellowish green shoots of *Cornus stolonifera* 'Flaviramea' (yellow dogwood), and they will draw nothing but admiration from onlookers.

But we must not forget the evergreen species. Even those of us who prefer the glorious autumn colours and naked winter bark, will not dispute that evergreen foliage gives visual depth, and a feeling of hope in the garden during winter. Add to this the advantage of winter leaves affording some protection to other plants, and we can only be drawn to the conclusion that evergreens are a necessity rather than a luxury.

In most cases, winter flowers are a welcome enough pleasure, but when you combine them with a delicious fragrance, the enjoyment really is doubled. Several excellent winter-flowering shrubs are also rated highly for their scent, and these include *Chimonanthus praecox* (winter sweet), *Daphne mezereum* (mezereon), *Lonicera fragrantissima* (winter honeysuckle), *Sarcococca confusa* (Christmas box) and *Viburnum farreri*.

Finally, a few of the shrubs mentioned in this chapter are being included for their beauty of berry. In most instances the berries will not have appeared for the first time in winter; rather they are the hangers-on from autumn. Nevertheless, they are included because of their provision of colour for the greater part of our coldest season.

ABELIOPHYLLUM

Here we have a really beautiful shrub from the Far East. It gives of its best when positioned near a wall that faces south or west, so facilitating the sun's heat to ripen the wood. Otherwise it makes an excellent shrub for training on a trellis or wire against the house. Fortunately it will more than likely succeed in any reasonably good garden soil. The faintly scented winter blooms last for several weeks.

A. distichum. As its leaves fall in autumn, the stems are already covered with tiny purple buds. These spring into life during mid-winter as blooms shaped like those of a forsythia, only creamy white tinged with pink. Flower arrangers can make good use of these as they last reasonably well in water. Height and spread: around 1.2 m (4 ft).

CELASTRUS (CLIMBING BITTERSWEET)

Not really a climber, more of a shrub with a twining habit. It will climb a wall well, but requires the added support of wire or trellis. Fences, tree stumps, arches and pergolas have all been enchanced by having this Far Eastern shrub growing along them. The starry greenish summer flowers are inconspicuous. The freely produced fruits which follow are the plant's main attraction. Celastrus will grow best in well-drained, non-chalky soils.

C. orbiculatus. This climbs vigorously, up and out to about 9m (30ft). The seedheads, which are similar to those of *Euonymus europaeus* (spindle tree), consist of small brown pods that split open to reveal a yellow lining and bright red seeds. Although the seeds first appear in autumn, this shrub is often planted for its eye-catching clusters decorating the bare, thorny, twining shoots.

CHIMONANTHUS (WINTER SWEET)

A small group of deciduous and evergreen shrubs originally from China. The one species most commonly seen is grown predominantly for the sweetly fragrant flowers on bare light brown branches. A chalky soil, in the protection of a south- or west-facing wall is the ideal, but ordinarily any well-drained soil and a sheltered site will do.

C. praecox (syn. *C. fragrans*). Height and spread: 3m (10ft). Although the pale yellow flowers are 2cm (¾in) across, when seen from a distance they are quite inconspicuous. It is the strong fragrance which is the main appeal of this plant. Flower arrangers make use regularly of its offering; indeed, a few sprigs will fill a room with delicious scent in a very short time.

CORNUS (DOGWOOD, CORNEL)

We have already looked at tree and shrubby forms for their autumn colour but some of the most spectacular winter stems are supplied by young shoots of dogwood. All types grown for this purpose succeed in partial shade and in most soils, including chalky, wet and waterlogged conditions. Pruning is crucial

with these shrubs if the stems are to be at their best in winter. Each spring all stems should be cut back hard to within a few inches of the ground. Throughout the following summer and autumn young growths will be produced, with good leaf coverage. During autumn the leaves will fall to reveal the fantastic spears of colour.

C. alba. A quick-growing deciduous shrub which, if left to its own devices, may grow up to around 3m (10ft). Its suckering habit makes it impossible to quantify its potential spread. Small yellow-white flowers are produced in early summer, and some reasonably good autumn leaf tints can be expected. But the winter stems are all important here, and the best forms to go for are 'Elegantissima', scarlet stems; 'Sibirica', coral red stems; and 'Spaethii', plum crimson stems. (Do not prune this last form quite so severely – it is not such a robust variety.)

C. stolonifera. Very similar in most respects to *C. alba*. Dull red bark is revealed in winter, except in the form 'Flaviramea' (yellow dogwood), which has bright green-yellow winter bark.

COTONEASTER

Several tree and shrub forms have already been discussed for their autumn merits, but one form is recommended for its persistent clusters of berries, which first appear at the end of summer, and remain well into winter. Cultural instructions are simple, as almost any position is suitable, including sunny sites and dry soils.

C. horizontalis (fish bone cotoneaster). This is probably the best known of all cotoneaster species, invaluable for north and east walls, excellent on banks, and rich in autumn leaf tints and persistent bright red winter berries. Its ground-hugging habit makes it ideal for ground cover. Height: 60cm (2ft). Spread: 1.8–2.1m (6–7ft).

A close-up of the lovely creamy-white, often yellow-tinged bark
of *Betula costata*.

DAPHNE

A group of evergreen and deciduous shrubs originally from Europe and Asia. The flowers are small, quite strongly coloured and deliciously fragrant. Daphnes are hardy and easy to grow – give them a sunny or partially shaded spot in any well-drained soil, even those containing chalk.

D. mezereum (mezereon). A small, upright shrub reaching an ultimate height of 1.5m (5ft), with a spread of 60–120cm (2–4ft). Star-shaped mauve-pink flowers appear in dense clusters on leafless stems during midwinter. Small scarlet berries follow, and these are poisonous.

D. odora. A slightly bigger evergreen plant, with a height and spread of 1.5–1.8m (5–6ft). The scented purple-pink blooms are produced from winter and last well into spring. In severe winters some stems may suffer, so it is always wise to plant this species in a sheltered spot.

ELAEAGNUS

A small group of shrubs, two species of which are extremely useful in the winter garden for their display of variegated evergreen leaves. These are not demanding shrubs as far as soil and site are concerned. They are also tolerant of shade, wind and seaside exposure, and are ideal for use as screens or informal hedges.

E. × ebbingei. A fast-growing hybrid reaching a height and spread of 3–4.5m (10–15ft), with leaves that have a white down over the dark green upper surface, and a scaly silver reverse. Small silver flowers are borne in late autumn, and these are sometimes followed by tiny oval red or orange fruits.

E. pungens. This is a tough, occasionally thorned, smaller species, reaching a height and spread of 2.4–3.6m (8–12ft). The leathery leaves are glossy green on the top surface, dull white beneath. Best forms for adding leaf colour to the winter garden are 'Macu-lata', leaves splashed with deep yellow, and 'Variegata', with narrow creamy yellow margins to the leaves.

ERICA (HEATH, HEATHER)

In their natural habitat, heaths and heathers grow in conditions which range from wet, even boggy areas, to exposed windswept mountainsides and moorlands (which dry out in the summer months). The majority of ericas require an acid-based soil. But fortunately for us winter flower lovers who garden with soil containing chalk, our choice rests predominantly with the winter-blooming types below. These plants are becoming more and more popular, mainly because there are so many varieties, and all fairly quick to establish. The use of heathers in the garden can vary from planting small groups along the front of shrub borders or beds, beds consisting entirely of heathers with a few carefully selected and sited dwarf or slow-growing conifers to add some height, a rock garden or, perhaps best of all, a separate heather garden. Ground cover is another bonus when growing heathers: because they are mostly low-growing shrubs which form rounded, spreading mounds only 30–45cm (12–18in) high, they are perfect for covering the soil and smothering annual weed seedlings which dare to germinate. Many sloping grass banks which are difficult to maintain can be planted with heathers. With a few specimen shrubs and rocks (to provide additional, attractive features), a troublesome area can be transformed into one requiring low maintenance.

E. carnea (syn. *E. herbacea*). A fully hardy species, growing to a height of 30cm (12in), and a spread of 60cm (24in). Leaves can vary from light green to bronze or yellow, depending on variety. The flowers which appear from late autumn to mid-spring are available in a number of shades. Some of the best are: 'Aurea', deep pink flowers and golden foliage; 'King George', rose pink flowers and green foliage; 'Myretoun Ruby', ruby red flowers and dark green leaves; 'Pink Spangles', pink flowers and mid-green leaves; 'Springwood Pink', bright pink blooms and green leaves: 'Springwood White', white flowers and bright green leaves; and 'Vivellii', carmine flowers and bronze leaves.

E. × darleyensis. A hybrid between *E. carnea* and *E. mediterranea*. This will grow to a height of 60cm (2ft), and a spread of 90cm (3ft) or more. The blooms appear first in mid-winter, and last until late spring. The young shoots are often creamy white or pink in spring before turning to their usual mid-green shade. Varieties to look for are: 'Arthur Johnson', rose-pink; 'Darley Dale', pale pink; and 'Silberschmelze' (often seen as 'Molten Silver', 'Silver Bells' or 'Silver Beads'), with silver-white flowers.

E. mediterranea (syn. *E. erigena)*. This is the odd plant out. It can reach a height of 2.4–3m (8–10ft), and spread out to 1.2m (4ft). Flowers appear from mid-winter until early summer. It has been known to suffer in harsh winters, so some protection, such as that afforded by a south- or west-facing wall, would be beneficial. Some of the best varieties are: 'Brightness', purple-red blooms and dark green leaves: 'Irish Dusk', deep salmon flower buds open to clear pink blooms with light grey leaves; and 'W. T. Rackliff', pure white flowers with emerald green leaves.

EUONYMUS

Two species have already been discussed for their autumn beauty. Whilst these are valuable for the larger garden, there are a number of evergreen species which are gaining more rapidly in popularity because of their compact growth and, often, attractive variegated foliage. Any soil, even chalk, will do.

E. fortunei (syn. *E. radicans*). This species has two different types of growth. The juvenile form has small, glossy leaves, while the adult foliage is perhaps twice the size. Height and spread of shrub: 1.5–2.1m (5–7ft). There are a couple of particularly attractive forms, both of which have variegated evergreen leaves which provide splashes of colour in the winter garden: 'Emerald Gaiety', whose round grey-green leaves have a creamy white margin, and 'Emerald 'n' Gold', with green, gold and pink-tinged leaves.

E. japonicus. Rather larger, this will reach an eventual height of 3–3.6m (10–12ft), with a spread of around 1.5m (5ft). This species is often regarded as the brightest of all – in leaf – and, although quite hardy, young potted forms can be used as temporary indoor foliage plants. 'Albomarginatus' has green leaves margined white; 'Ovatus Aureus' is dark green with thick golden yellow margins.

FATSIA (FATSIA, CASTOR OIL SHRUB)

As this is popular as a house plant we could be forgiven for thinking it a tender plant, but in fact it is quite hardy. It prefers a partially shaded sheltered spot, and will thrive in any reasonable garden soil. It is particularly successful as a seaside bush, or as a specimen shrub in a town garden.

F. japonica. This plant has wide-spreading branches and fascinating large, glossy leaves – more than 30cm (12in) across – arranged like the fingers of a hand. It qualifies, too, as a seasonal flowerer. Large, globular clusters of off-white blooms are at their best in late autumn, and last well into winter. Height and spread: 3–4.5m (10–15ft). The form 'Variegata' has white-edged leaves.

GARRYA (TASSEL BUSH)

A small group of evergreen shrubs, only one species of which is generally available. Garryas are grown for their attractive hanging

Grown chiefly for its polished red-brown winter bark, *Prunus serrula* originally came from China.

catkins. Male and female flowers are carried on separate plants, but the males are more ornamental, and consequently more frequently seen. These shrubs are easy to grow in any well-drained garden soil; they flower best in full sun, but will tolerate shade. Where possible, plant against a south-facing wall.

G. elliptica. The glossy evergreen foliage is a dramatic feature in itself, and able to withstand the onslaught of city smoke and dirt. The catkins of the male plants are long, slender and silvery green, appearing in mid-winter and lasting well into spring. Sometimes they are so numerous they practically cover the whole plant. They turn pale yellow as the pollen is released. Height and spread: around 3.6m (12ft).

HAMAMELIS (WITCH HAZEL)

Some forms of this attractive group of shrubs have already been covered for their autumn merits, but it is their winter and spring flower performance for which they receive most recognition. Give them a lime-free soil, preferably heavily enriched with peat or leaf-mould to retain moisture, so encouraging strong growth.

H. × intermedia. A fairly vigorous form, with a height and spread of around 1.8–3m (6–10ft). The flowers are variable, from medium to large, and are yellow tinted with copper. There are several excellent forms: 'Jelena' (syn. 'Copper Beauty') has coppery bronze blooms.

H. japonica (Japanese witch hazel). Strongly scented lemon yellow blooms are held on branches 2.4–3m (8–10ft) high. The form 'Sulphurea', as the name implies, produces pale, sulphur yellow flowers. 'Zuccariniana' (usually the last of the witch hazels to flower), is similar, but the blooms are slightly smaller.

H. mollis (Chinese witch hazel). This is probably the best known and most widely planted species. It will eventually reach 1.8–2.4m (6–8ft) in height and spread. The blooms, which often appear in thick clusters during the early part of winter, are rich golden yellow, flushed red at the base. They have a delicate fragrance, too. There are several forms worth seeking out. 'Brevipetala' has small, later-opening blooms which range in colour from a deep golden yellow to a light orange. By contrast, 'Coombe Wood' has larger flowers than the type, and the shrub is also more wide-spreading. 'Goldcrest' is probably the last form of *H. mollis* to flower, with heavily scented attractive golden yellow blooms, tinged with pink (giving an overall orange appearance). 'Pallida' on the other hand has pale lemon yellow blooms.

HEDERA (IVY)

Few plants rival the hederas for ease of cultivation; indeed, they survive neglect that would spell death to most garden plants. This, and the introduction of modern and varied kinds, explain the dramatic rise in popularity of ivies over the last 20 years or so. Too many gardeners still think of ivy as a tree-damaging weed, or more recently as a house plant. But a carefully chosen form, if pruned properly, is a reliable and often colourful climber – the variegated forms will add a touch of sunshine to the winter garden. Neither trees, nor brickwork (if it is in good condition), will be damaged, but the ivy should be pruned yearly to reduce its weight on the supporting structure. Increasing use is made of them today for ground cover as well as in their well-established use as climbers. The leaf shape of the many varieties is often quite different (like *Euonymus fortunei*, there is 'juvenile' and 'adult' foliage). The extent to which these climbers flourish in woodlands, specially on chalky soil, is a clue to their needs. But remember, to maintain good leaf variegation, some exposure to the sun is desirable. Out of the 15 species known, I regard just three as being of particular merit in the winter garden.

H. canariensis (Canary Island ivy). Single stems will extend to 4.5–6m (15–10ft). It's a handsome, quick-growing species, but may suffer slightly in harsh winters. The large, leathery leaves are practically heart-shaped, bright green in summer, turning bronzy in winter. The form 'Gloire de Marengo' (syn. 'Variegata'), produces leaves that are dark green in the centre, merging through silver to a white margin.

H. colchica (Persian Ivy) This is larger, with stems reaching out 6–9m (20–30ft). The plain green leaves are not spectacular, but the best form is 'Dentata Variegata', the leaves of which are marked with cream-yellow and pale green.

H. helix (common ivy). A British species, and the one usually seen clothing tree stems in woods. 'Goldheart' (syn. 'Jubilee') is the best form for winter colour. The small, tapering dark green leaves each have a central golden blotch. Another excellent variety to brighten up your winter garden is 'Buttercup', with all-over golden yellow leaves.

JASMINUM (JASMINE)

The summer-flowering white *J. officinale* is a climber, but the species of interest to us here is the yellow, winter-flowering shrub. Despite the intensity and profusion of bloom, this is an undemanding plant growing in any ordinary soil and thriving against a north-facing wall. Some support for the branches is desirable if you wish the plant to attain a height above 1.2m (4ft). Otherwise, allow the branches to trail down – possibly to cover unsightly tree stumps or manhole covers!

J. nudiflorum (winter jasmine). The leafless green stems, perhaps 3m (10ft) or more in length, bear bright yellow star-shaped flowers from late autumn until early spring. The blooms, unfortunately, are susceptible to damage by cold winds.

LONICERA (HONEYSUCKLE)

A large group of evergreen and deciduous flowering shrubs and climbers. The flowers, specially those of the climbers, are deliciously fragrant. Some of the shrubby varieties are useful for hedging. Our native *L. periclymenum* (honeysuckle or woodbine), is a climber and bears summer flowers. Two less commonly seen bush forms produce excellent, fragrant, winter blooms. Any ordinary well-drained garden soil will do, in sun or partial shade.

L. fragrantissima. A semi-evergreen shrub originally from China, with an eventual height and spread of 1.8m (6ft). Masses of highly scented creamy white flowers, arrange in pairs, are carried along the branches from late winter until spring.

L. standishii. This rather gaunt species will also reach 1.8m (6ft), and is fully deciduous. The main difference between the two species is that *L. standishii* has small bristles on the leaf stalks.

MAHONIA

A group of hardy evergreen shrubs, related to the berberis and grown for their glossy green foliage and bell-shaped or round winter and spring flowers. These shrubs are best seen as specimen plants on their own. The foliage is sought after by flower arrangers during the autumn-winter period. The plants are not fussy as to soil, and they will withstand shade. Once established mahonias require little attention.

M. bealei. Originally from China, this will reach a height and spread of 1.8–2.4m (6–8ft). Spread: 1.8–1.4m (6–8ft). Spikes of lemon yellow blooms open in clusters at the tips of the stems, from early winter.

M. 'Charity'. This is my favourite. The scented, deep yellow blooms often open in autumn, and last well into spring. Height: 2.4–3m (8–10ft). Spread: 1.8–2.4m (6–8ft).

The vividly coloured red and yellow seeds of *Celastrus orbiculatus* (climbing bittersweet).

M. japonica. Pale primrose yellow blooms in long, narrow clusters have a lily-of-the-valley fragrance. They show from late autumn until mid-winter. Height: 2.4–3m (8–10ft). Spread: 2.4–3.6m (8–12ft).

PACHYSANDRA

This small group of hardy, evergreen creeping shrubs is excellent for suppressing weed growth. Their dense heads of leaves block out all light, and weeds cannot generally break through this most effective ground cover. These shade lovers are not frequently seen; indeed, you may even have some difficulty in finding them in your local garden shops. The reason for this, perhaps, is that the flowers are small and relatively insignificant. Pachysandras succeed best in moist, non-chalky soils. They do not like a position in full sun.

P. terminalis (Japanese spurge). Foliage a deep to mid-green covers the plants on stems reaching only 30cm (12in) in height, with a spread of 45–60cm (18–24in). In late winter, and into spring, the tiny petal-less greeny white blooms appear on short stalks. The leaves are certainly the main feature, and a winter scene can be improved with the form 'Variegata', with white edges to the diamond-shaped leaves.

PERNETTYA (PRICKLY HEATH)

This, I believe, is one of the best berrying shrubs. Its low-growing habit and small, spiky evergreen leaves make it a highly decorative feature of the autumn and winter garden. Small cream flowers appear in spring, and they are followed by lovely berries in large clusters. Although the fruits first appear in autumn, they are retained until the end of winter. Being a relative of the heather and rhododendron, an acid soil is essential – add peat to the hole at planting time. A sunny or partially shaded position will do.

P. mucronata. Originally from South America, this species produces pale pink berries. Height and spread: 60–90cm (2–3ft). There are several forms with different coloured fruits: 'Alba', pure white; 'Bell's Seedling', dark red; and 'Lilacina', lilac.

RHODODENDRON

This is a large group of trees and shrubs, which are planted extensively to provide our gardens with some colour during spring. Certainly wild forms, albeit introduced ones, light up our countryside from mid-spring. But any tome extolling the virtues of shrubs with winter colour, and which omitted the rhododendron, would be sadly lacking. The flowering period of this genus is exceptionally long: *R. mucronulatum* flowers from the beginning of winter, while *R. auriculatum* does not bloom until high summer. Besides the 500 or so species that occur naturally throughout the world, there are innumerable hybrids and varieties. A great many of the natural species are too large and cumbersome to be accommodated happily in the small garden of today; although some merely form small mounds, or creep along the ground, rather more become tall bushes, or even trees 18m (60ft) in height. This is why breeders are always introducing dwarf hybrids with larger and more colourful flowers which are specially suited to the smaller plot of land. All rhododendrons demand acid soil, and where the ideal conditions do not occur naturally, it is well worth creating them artificially, by lacing the hole at planting time with a suitable humus-rich mixture, or by using a prepared lime-free compost in an urn, vase or tub. Any traces of chalk in the soil will soon turn the leaves pale and yellow. Although in the wild rhododendrons grow in shady and woodland conditions, nearly all types will stand full sun. An important tip here though: never let the soil become dry. Ensure good moisture at the roots by

Bare dogwood stems in winter are a familiar sight. Here is *Cornus alba* 'Spaethii'.

watering during dry periods, and by regularly mulching with compost, straw, manure, or a mixture of the three. In our winter garden we must be very choosy for, it has to be said, there are a great many rhododendrons that do not warrant space in the garden. A great deal of emphasis is put on their foliage in the winter garden. The evergreen forms can, indeed, provide dense greenery and be desirable for this reason. But the leaves are generally 'just green', and it is my view that we should perhaps be thinking of introducing types with flowers of vivid colours. I have, therefore, limited my selection here to those with warming blooms to brighten the dull days of winter. They also, incidentally, enhance the already accepted valuable foliage!

R. arboreum (tree rhododendron). A large evergreen shrub, with a height and spread of up to 12m (40ft), and originally from the Himalayas. The blooms, which appear from mid-winter onwards, vary in colour from pale pink to blood red. It is a natural species which – with another parent – has given rise to many hybrids. One such offspring is 'Nobleanum' (where the other parent is *R. caucasicum*), with clusters of rose pink, funnel-shaped flowers. They are even more attractive in the bud stage, being brilliant scarlet. 'Nobleanum Album' is similar, but produces white blooms.

R. 'Christmas Cheer'. I am now going to dispel the myth regarding this old and hardy evergreen hybrid: it misses Christmas by months even in the northern hemisphere, and does not flower until late winter or early spring. A mild season will, however, encourage mid-winter blooms. It is certainly worth the wait. Its dazzling blush pink blooms are darker in bud. Height and spread: 1.2–1.8m (4–6ft).

R. mucronulatum. Probably the best known winter-flowering rhododendron. It is perfectly hardy, and produces masses of intense rose-purple trumpet-shaped blooms from early winter. This species is semi-deciduous, only really losing all of its leaves after prolonged heavy frosts. But very shortly the flower buds begin swelling, and are soon showing some colour. Height: 1.8m (6ft). Spread: 60–90cm (2–3ft).

R. 'Praecox'. Coming in towards the end of winter, but still within the limits of our subject, is this hardy, semi-evergreen hybrid. Although most of the aromatic (when crushed) leaves fall in late autumn, the numerous small bright lilac-pink blooms take their place beautifully. The opening buds are, at first, a reddish purple. This form enjoys a fully sunny position, and will even tolerate a little lime in the soil. Height and spread: around 1.5m (5ft).

RUBUS (ORNAMENTAL BRAMBLE)

This genus boasts the blackberry, raspberry and Japanese wineberry among its fruiting species, but like the dogwoods discussed earlier in this chapter, there are two forms that are widely grown for their glorious naked winter stems. They will grow in any reasonable garden soil, in sun or semi-shade.

R. biflorus. A vigorous species with prickly winter stems that are basically green, but covered with a vivid white waxy bloom. Small, edible yellow (but insignificant) fruits are produced in autumn. Height:1.8–2.4m (6–8ft). Spread: 1.5–1.8m (5–6ft).

R. cockburnianus (whitewashed bramble). Another deciduous species, with dramatic, arching branches that are white tinged blue in winter. Same height and spread as the former species. To encourage new white-covered stems every year, remove all old branches in early spring.

SARCOCOCCA

Small, slow-growing evergreen shrubs originally from the Far East. They are grown both for their attractive green foliage, and highly scented white blooms. While growing well in any light soil, these shrubs have a particular liking for a peaty or acid soil. They are excellent shade plants, and will withstand being sited under large trees.

S. confusa (Christmas box, sweet box). The glossy green leaves – long, slender and pointed – are accompanied in late winter by small creamy white blooms with a powerful fragrance. Height and spread: around 1.2m (4ft).

S. hookerana digyna. Scented white winter blooms on this shrub which originates in China. Its ultimate height is 1.8m (6ft), but with a spread of only 90–120cm (3–4ft).

S. humilis. A suckering shrub, which will eventually form a dense thicket about 60cm (2ft) high. The glossy dark evergreen leaves make excellent weed-preventing ground cover. The late winter blooms, once again sweetly scented, are white with pale pink centres.

VIBURNUM

On p.46 we looked at viburnums recommended for their autumn colour. Here we will discuss those with winter flowers. The same cultural conditions apply.

V. × bodnantense. A vigorous garden hybrid with stiff, upright stems carrying highly fragrant white-pink flower heads from early winter. Not a small shrub, it has a height and spread of around 3–3.6m (10–12ft). The form 'Dawn' is most widely seen, the blooms of which are a deeper pink, and last almost until spring.

V. × burkwoodii. A smaller, evergreen garden hybrid, reaching a height of 2.4m (8ft), and a spread of 2.4–3m (8–10ft). Dark green leaves are accompanied from mid-winter until late spring by waxy, sweet-scented white blooms that are pink in bud.

V. farreri (syn V. fragrans). Originally from China, this species will reach a height and spread of 2.7–3.6m (9–12ft). It is highly acclaimed for its many clusters of pink buds opening to white flower heads from late autumn.

V. tinus (laurustinus). This European species is evergreen with mid- to deep green leaves. White, pink-budded flower clusters are carried at the ends of the shoots from mid-autumn until late spring (over half of the year). Height: 2.1–3m (7–10ft). Spread: up to 2.1m (7ft). The form 'Eve Price' is excellent, with pink-tinged blooms.

CHAPTER NINE

BORDER PLANTS IN WINTER

So far we have not had to search far to find a wealth of colourful plant material. Each chapter has opened up a new area of plants, and my problem has been deciding which plants to leave out! However, we now come to the subject of perennials in winter, and it is one area that is rather lacking in variety. Flower colour is reasonably well represented (except for bright red), and there is a good range of sizes available to us, from the tiny *Hepatica nobilis* at 8cm (3in) in height, to the large-leaved *Bergenia* 'Ballawley Hybrid' with foliage 35cm (14in) across. To give you an idea of the quantity of border plants available with winter merit, there are around only a quarter of the number of shrubs! The following plants should give you plenty of interest during the coldest months.

BERGENIA (ELEPHANT'S EARS)

Where there are gaps in the border, and regardless of soil and situation, you could do no better than to grow one or more of the bergenias. These large-leaved beauties are relatively trouble-free, give an excellent show of flowers in mid-winter or spring (depending on variety), and give practically year-round ground cover. Interestingly, the flowers appear as the old leaves begin to fade, and by the time the flowers are over, there is a new, fresh crop of glossy green leaves. Where autumn and winter colour is concerned, these plants are dual purpose, for their leaves often have reddish tints as they come to the end of their useful life. The roots of these plants are very near to the surface of the soil, so provide little competition for the deeper roots of the shrubs and trees around which

they grow. However, any hoeing or surface cultivation near them should be curtailed, otherwise much irreparable damage could be done to the roots. The flowers, when they first open, are rather like hyacinths, in a closely packed stumpy spike, but after a few days they open out and become branched. Bergenias will grow in moist, almost boggy areas, out in the open garden under full sun, or under trees where it is fairly dry.

B. 'Abendglut' (syn. *B.* 'Evening Glow') A hybrid whose red-purple blooms do not appear until spring. But in winter the large, round leaves take on a nice coppery colour. Height and planting distance: 23cm (9in).

B. 'Ballawley Hybrid'. Extra large leaves, perhaps 35cm (14in) across, turn bronze in winter. Fuchsia-red flowers appear in spring. Height and planting distance: 40cm (16in).

B. crassifolia. This species is the best bergenia for flowering in winter. Its pale pink heads of bell-shaped blooms are carried on 30cm (12in) high stalks between mid-winter and mid-spring. Planting distance: 30cm.

HELLEBORUS (HELLEBORE)

This small genus of winter-flowering evergreen and deciduous perennials contains the popular Christmas and Lenten roses, and while the plants are hardy enough to be grown out of doors, they are often spoiled by the frost and winds unless some protection is given. Consequently, these plants are not really suitable for open or exposed beds and borders. However in a sheltered spot, perhaps among shrubs, they will provide much interest and subtle colour during the

The long-lasting bright red berries of the fishbone cotoneaster (*C. horizontalis*).

winter months. The flowers are long-lasting (even when cut for indoor decoration). They are white, cream, green, pink, purple; some are heavily spotted, others at any one time may be of two or more colours, fading from one to another. They grow best in moist, well-drained rich soils, preferably in partial shade. They should, ideally, be left after planting, as they bitterly resent disturbance.

H. atrorubens. The dark green leaves mainly fall from the plant in winter, leaving room for the deep plum purple cup-shaped blooms with yellow anthers. The flowers keep up their show until mid-spring. Height: 25cm (10in). Planting distance: 45cm (18in).

H. corsicus (syn *H. argutifolius*). The mid green to pale green leaves of this species from Corsica are evergreen. The later winter blooms are cup-shaped and yellow-green. Height and planting distance: 60cm (24in).

H. foetidus (stinking hellebore). Shiny, dark green, deeply cut leaves clothe this species throughout the year. But from late winter until late spring the yellow-green purple-edged flowers provide much interest. Despite its name, this plant is not markedly pungent. Height and planting distance: 60cm (24in).

H. niger (Christmas rose). There may have been a time when this species lived up to its common name, but nowadays it scarcely applies. Not that this really matters, for it is still the depths of winter when the first saucer-shaped white, yellow-centred blooms appear among the dark evergreen leaves. Height and planting distance: 45cm (18in).

H. orientalis (Lenten rose). The forms of this species are much more adaptable and reliable than the others so far mentioned. From mid-winter, for about two months, the blooms come in a colour range from white, through shades of pink to plum purple. Much like the bergenias, the leaves thoughtfully disappear to make way for the blooms, and come back when the blooms start to fade.

Height: around 50cm (20in). Planting distance: 45cm (18in).

H. viridis (green hellebore). This usually opens its nodding pale green cup-shaped blooms in mid-winter. A native species to Britain, it prefers a slightly chalky soil. Height: 30cm (12in). Planting distance: 45cm (18in).

HEPATICA

A small group of hardy plants, best suited to rockeries. In such a position these are particularly welcome, as they come into flower before the late winter charms of aubrieta, alyssum and arabis. Hepaticas form little mounds, and thrive best in shade, in retentive acid or peaty soils with a cool root run. As they are versatile enough to tolerate a sunny spot, it is surprising that they are not seen more often.

H. nobilis (syn. *H.triloba, Anemone hepatica*). This is the species you are most likely to come across. The small blue star-shaped flowers are carried on stalks only 8cm (3in) high, between mid-winter and mid-spring. White and pink strains are available, but you may have to search hard to find them. Spread: up to 30cm (12in).

PRIMULA

A large group of plants, with some 500 species, comprising deciduous and evergreen, hardy and tender perennials. This generous genus provides us with some of the most attractive flowers for growing in greenhouses, rock gardens, borders, woodlands or waterside. Familiar wild flowers in this group include *P. veris* (cowslip) and *P. elatior* (oxlip). The following winter-flowering outdoor types require a humus-rich, well-drained soil, and are suited to growing in a rock garden.

P. allionii. This is really seen at its best in an unheated greenhouse (which, if devoted mainly to rock plants, is termed an 'alpine

Add a touch of sunshine to your winter garden by planting
Elaeagnus pungens 'Maculata'.

house'). Prolonged, wet winters have seen the demise of many rockery plants, so the drier confines of a greenhouse provide just the right protection. If grown in such a way, the compost within the pot should be gritty, with some lime and humus added. Respectable colour, however, can be had from specimens grown outdoors. This delightful species forms a hummock of sticky, mid-green leaves. From late winter these may be completely hidden by the blooms. which vary from purple and rose red to white. Height: 8cm (3in). Spread: 15–25cm (6–10in).

P. edgeworthii (syn. *P. winteri*) The grey-green leaves are accompanied, from mid-winter, by pale lavender flowers, each with a yellow centre. Height: 10cm (4in). Spread: 23cm (9in).

P. juliae. This species forms a flat mat of creeping shoots, with pale green round leaves. The small red-purple blooms, with yellow centres, appear from late winter until late spring. Height: 8cm (3in). Spread: 30cm (12in).

P. vulgaris (common primrose). This native primula is a familiar sight in woodlands and hedgerows during late winter and spring. It will enjoy a slightly wetter soil than the others. A rosette of green leaves is upstaged by the primrose yellow blooms with deeper coloured centres. Height: 15cm (6in). Spread: 23cm (9in). The Polyanthus primroses have been largely bred from this species. These showy plants are ideal for bedding. Usually raised from seed in late spring, they are grown on and planted outdoors in autumn. They make most attractive displays of cream, yellow, pink, red, crimson and purple from late winter until late spring. They may reach a height and spread of 30cm (12in). Unfortunately the bright early season flower buds are loved by birds (woodpigeons and finches are particularly troublesome). Generally, a few strands of black cotton suspended at flower height will deter these marauding creatures. After flowering do not

let the plants dry out, otherwise blooming the following year will be seriously affected.

P. 'Wanda'. This is a hybrid of *P. juliae*, and is one of the most vivid and long-lasting of all winter flowers. It bears a profusion of bright claret blooms. Height: 10cm (4in). Spread: 30cm (12in).

PULMONARIA (LUNGWORT)

A small group of dwarf-growing perennials, growing best in moist soil. They also like a partially shaded situation. The forms discussed here have green leaves with white spots or markings. An unusual but most pleasing characteristic of these plants is that the flowers open pink and turn blue with age. A not-so-pleasant characteristic is that the small hairs on the stems and leaves sometimes cause irritation to the skin.

P. officinalis (Jerusalem cowslip, spotted dog). This late winter bloomer has narrow white-spotted leaves, and produces funnel-shaped purple-blue flowers. Height and planting distance: 30cm (12in).

P. saccharata. With this we have narrow bright green leaves marbled with silver-white. Pink funnel-shaped blooms open just before those of *P. officinalis* but soon change to sky blue. The best varieties are 'Bowles Red', with rose pink blooms, and 'Pink Dawn', pale pink. Height and planting distance: 30cm (12in).

VIOLA (GARDEN PANSY)

We discussed *V. odorata* (sweet violet) on p. 54. This produces its main flush of blooms during late winter and early spring, with a secondary flush in autumn. However, there is one further species which produces several winter-flowering forms. The same cultural conditions apply.

V. × wittrockiana (syn. *V. tricolor hortensis*). A strain of semi-tender annual and biennial hybrids, basically similar to natural violets but more vigorous and with larger flowers. For the winter-flowering pansies, mild and protected sites are best. If these are provided blooms can be expected to continue well into spring. An early summer sowing will provide blooms the following winter. These types are usually sold as mixtures, such as 'Supremo Early' and 'Floral Dance Mixed', where shades of red, bronze, yellow, blue, white, deep rose and purple (all with dark central blotches) are available. But a few varieties with separate colours can be grown. Try 'Coronation Gold', golden yellow; 'Crimson Queen', velvety-red; 'Fire Beacon', red-orange and 'Mount Everest', pure white. Height and spread: 15–23cm (6–9in).

If you have an acid, or peat-based soil, you could liven up your
winter garden by planting a selection of heathers.

CHAPTER TEN

BULBS IN WINTER

In Chapter Five, I said that the spring-flowering types are the most commonly seen. These, of course, include narcissi, tulips, crocuses and hyacinths, and most welcome they are, too. But there are several narcissus and crocus forms which flower a month or two before spring. Their importance is twofold. First they provide vivid colour only a few inches off the ground (where much winter colour is high on shrubs and trees), and second, they seem to prolong the spring season by giving the impression that it starts early! There are other familiar names in the world of winter bulbs: cyclamen, *Eranthis hyemalis* (winter aconite), *Galanthus nivalis* (snowdrop) and the miniature irises.

With careful selection of bulbs, a feast of winter colour is available to us – except brilliant red.

CHIONODOXA
(GLORY OF THE SNOW)

A group of very pretty, hardy Mediterranean bulbous plants with short sprays of starry flowers from mid-winter. They grow well in any ordinary, well-drained soil outside, or they may be planted in pots for growing in an unheated greenhouse. They all have strap-shaped and blunt-tipped, mid-green leaves, often bronze tinted when young.

C. gigantea (syn. *C. grandiflora*). The flower spike carries several pale blue star-shaped blooms, each with a small white centre. Height: 15 cm (6 in). Planting distance: 8–10 cm (3–4 in).

C. luciliae. Flowers similar to *C. gigantea*, but of a lighter blue and slightly smaller. Height: 15 cm (6 in). Planting distance: 5–10 cm (2–4 in). 'Pink Giant' is a very lovely form with numerous pure pink blooms.

COLCHICUM

On p.57 we looked at two types of autumn-flowering colchicum. They are quite spectacular in autumn with their wineglass-shaped flowers, followed by the large floppy leaves. In fact, leaves are often regarded as the one disadvantage of colchicums. They grow rapidly, and may smother smaller plants. Certainly they look untidy when they are withering and dying. The autumn-flowering forms have mainly pink, lilac or mauve blooms. There is, however, one odd colchicum: it is a winter bloomer; it produces its leaves at the same time as the flowers, and its colour is yellow!

C. luteum. Originally from the Himalayas and Russia, this sets flower in mid-winter, and lasts until early spring. It's the only yellow form, reaching a height of 8–10 cm (3-4 in). Space plants 10–15 cm (4–6) apart. The leaves are mid-green throughout spring, and wither during the early part of summer.

CROCUS

Everyone knows the crocus, with its very showy white, lilac, purple or yellow blooms. We have already looked at one of the true autumn crocuses – now on to the larger, more familiar range of winter and early spring types. Most crocus species and varieties require a well-drained soil and a sunny position.

C. chrysanthus. This species hails from the warmer climes of Greece and Turkey.

Having said that, they are perfectly hardy in cooler zones. Golden yellow flowers 8cm (3in) high are produced from mid-winter. The main claim to fame of *C. chrysanthus*, though, is that is has been crossed with several other forms to provide numerous hybrids. Among the best are: 'Blue Bird', purplish blue and white; 'Blue Pearl', light blue; 'Cream Beauty', cream; 'E. A. Bowles', deep yellow with a bronze base; 'Lady Killer', purple-blue edged with white; 'Snow Bunting', white with a bronze base; and 'Zwanenburg Bronze', bright yellow inside the petals, heavily marked with bronze on the outside.

C. imperati. From early to mid-winter, cup-shaped flowers 8–10cm (3–4in) high are produced on this Italian species. The pretty blooms are buff outside, and lavender blue inside.

C. sieberi. Pale mauve blooms, yellow at the base, appear during mid- to late winter. Height: 8cm (3in). 'Hubert Edelstein' is probably the best form, with rose-lilac flowers.

C. tomasinianus. Towards the end of winter, narrow buds appear, displaying only the pale mauve exterior of the outer petals. They soon open to show the lilac inner petals. Height: 8cm (3in). The form 'Ruby Giant' has slightly larger, deep violet blooms.

CYCLAMEN

On p.58 the autumn-flowering *C. hederifolium* was discussed. There is also one equally prominent winter bloomer. A well-drained, humus-rich soil in a shady position is the ideal, although warm, sunny corners will be tolerated.

C. coum (syn. *C. vernum*). The kidney-shaped mid-green leaves are dark red below and sometimes marbled with silver above. Small pink, carmine or near-white flowers on 8cm (3in) stems appear from late autumn until early spring. The tubers should be set

between 10–15cm (4–6in) apart. This species is tiny – although sturdy – and really deserves to be grown in a choice corner of the rock garden, or at least in an area given over entirely to miniature plants and bulbs.

ERANTHIS (WINTER ACONITE)

One of the first flowers to open in winter out of doors. Not really a bulb, this group of plants grows from tuberous roots. Plant a patch of these little tubers in a shady bed or under deciduous shrubs, and you will be delighted by the carpet of yellow flowers. Eranthis are often planted with snowdrops, as they flower much at the same time. Any well-drained soil will do.

E. hyemalis. This is the most popular form. Lemon yellow flowers are set proud of an attractive collar of deep-cut mid-green bracts. Height: 10cm (4in). Set tubers 8cm (3in) apart. This species sets seed readily, and will soon spread beyond its allocated space if you are not careful.

E. × tubergenii. This is a less invasive hybrid, with larger, later and more dramatic rich yellow flowers than *E. hyemalis*. Height: 10cm (4in). Planting distance of tubers: 8–10cm (3–4in) apart.

GALANTHUS (SNOWDROP)

We have already looked at one autumn-flowering snowdrop. The winter types are often regarded as the 'curtain raisers of the year'. The common snowdrop is one plant we should all make room for in quantity, and no flower of the season speaks so strongly of winter. All forms are at home in woodland conditions, where they are sheltered throughout the year by leaves, moss, grass and so on. They contrast well with the trailing ivy, another common woodland dweller. Lovely as the common single and double snowdrops are, many other species and old garden varieties may be had from specialist growers,

The heavily-scented yellow blooms of *Hamamelis mollis* 'Goldcrest' (a form of Chinese witch hazel).

all currently enjoying a new surge of popularity among keen growers. At first glance, one snowdrop may look very much like another, but the subtle variations in flower shape, size and markings are fascinating. And, since flowering times vary, the more you have, the longer the snowdrop season will last: instead of a two or three week display, you can have flowers from the onset of winter until the middle of spring. Naturally, the less common types are rather more expensive, but then even two or three bulbs will, with correct treatment, soon increase. All forms enjoy the well-drained conditions that prevail among the roots of trees and shrubs. However, do improve the impoverished soil in such situations, thoroughly mixing in some peat, well-rotted garden compost or (best of all) leaf-mould, plus a little long-lasting compound fertilizer.

G. elwesii (giant snowdrop). This species is larger than most. It will reach a height of 15–25cm (6–10in). Planting distance of bulbs: 10–20cm (4–8in). The large mid-winter white blooms are deep green on the inner petals.

G. nivalis (common snowdrop). A bulb native to Great Britain, this will reach 8–20cm (3–8in) in height, depending on soil and site. Planting distance: 8–15in (3–6in). The white flowers have green markings on the inner petals. The form 'Plenus' has double flowers, but somewhat less elegant than the species. 'S. Arnott' is often regarded as the best variety, having slightly larger, yet single, white blooms. 'Viridapicis' has green spots on the outer as well as the inner petals.

IPHEION (SPRING STARFLOWER, FLOWER-OF-THE-INCAS)

A small group of hardy bulbs from Central and South America, distantly related to the lily, but looking nothing like it! Spring is the main season for these, I will admit, but a mild spell in mid-winter will very often be suf-

ficient to encourage the delicate blooms to appear. Low-growing, easy-to-look-after subjects, ipheions will flourish in a sunny rockery, or at the front of a flower border. Each bulb sends up several flowering stalks. The bulbs and grass-like leaves have a faint garlic smell. The plants are generally trouble-free, provided the soil is kept free-draining.

I. uniflorum (syn. *Brodiaea uniflora, Tritelia uniflora*). The flowers are up to 5cm (2in) wide, and white to lavender. The most widely seen named variety is 'Wisley Blue', violet blue.

IRIS

A very large group of bulbous and rhizomatous plants, with sword-shaped leaves generally grey-green to a deep glossy green. The genus contains many of the most popular and useful of the garden plants that are commonly grown today. Of the rhizomatous types, the largest and most popular group is known as the bearded irises, which generally flower in early summer. Here, we are more interested in the bulbous types. Of these, there are many spring- and summer-flowering kinds, such as varieties of *I. xiphioides* (English irises) and *I. xiphium* (Spanish irises), and the hybrid Dutch irises (raised by crossing *I. tingitana* and *I. xiphium*). But there are some fascinating and spectacularly colourful winter-blooming types as well. Although hardy, these irises need some protection to prevent the blooms being spoiled by any prolonged wet and blowy winter weather, and are therefore best grown in a frame, or in pots in an unheated greenhouse. They can be grown for a number of years in pots if well cared for. However, the surest way of getting the best display from them is to buy and plant new bulbs each year – the earlier the better, as they really need to be potted in early autumn.

I. danfordiae. Originally from Turkey, this is probably the brightest of the winter irises, with its lemon yellow, honey-scented blooms on 10cm (4in) high stalks. They should be planted 5–10cm (2–4in) apart. The blooms appear from mid- to late winter. This species is difficult to keep for more than one year, as the flowering bulbs tend to split up into numerous smaller ones, none of which is sufficiently large to flower again for several years.

I. histrioides 'Major'. The only form of *I. histrioides* generally on offer. The first of the winter irises to flower, with sturdy 8cm (3in) high light blue blooms with yellow markings. The leaves are only 2.5cm (1in) high at flowering time, but by mid-spring will reach 45cm (18in). This form will survive all weathers, even heavy prolonged snow. It is an easy iris to grow, and one that usually multiplies readily and goes on flowering year after year. Planting distance: 5–10cm (2–4in).

I. reticulata. This winter bulb species is the most variable in colour. The blooms are more slender than those of *I. histrioides*, are carried on longer, 15cm (6in) high stems, and are violet-scented. They open a couple of weeks later, from mid- to late winter. The general colour is violet-purple splashed with gold, but 'Cantab' is pale blue with orange markings; 'Harmony' is sky blue with yellow markings; 'J. S. Dijt' is deep purple with orange markings; and 'Pauline' is violet-purple with white markings. Plant about 10cm (4in) apart.

I. unguicularis (syn. *I. stylosa*), (Algerian iris). This differs from most species by requiring poor but well-drained soil in a warm place, preferably under a south- or west-facing wall. Flowers are lilac with white and yellow markings, and quite fragrant. They will appear from early winter until early spring, in small flushes rather than continuous colour. However, after a poor summer, flowering may not begin until mid-winter. Flower arrangers make good use of the blooms, but there is one important tip to remember here: pull them while they are still in their bud stage; they will open indoors after only a few minutes. The roots are rhizomatous, not bulbous. Height: up to 45cm (18in). Planting distance: 40cm (15in).

LEUCOJUM (SNOWFLAKE)

Allied to the snowdrop is this small group of bulbous plants. Only three species are in general cultivation, and two of these are *L. aestivum* (summer snowflake) and *L. autumnale* (autumn snowflake), which both flower in their respective seasons. We are, therefore, interested in the remaining species. It is well-fitted to withstand the weather, but slugs love it. It seems to like cool positions best, such as may be found on the northern side of the garden. Also, it will thrive in quite damp, humus-laden soil. It resents disturbance, so once in the soil, leave it alone.

L. vernum. Strap-shaped mid-green leaves appear at the same time as the flowers, which are drooping, bell-shaped and white with green tips. Height: 20cm (8in). Planting distance: 8–10cm (3–4in). Useful for providing spots of low brightness from mid- to late winter.

NARCISSUS

The Royal Horticultural Society Classified List and International Register contains about 8000 named daffodil varieties – Wordsworth would have been in his element were he alive today! Botanically, all daffodils are part of a group of plants called narcissus. The trumpet narcissi, which have a central trumpet as long as, or longer than the surrounding petals, are what we regard as the common daffodil. These large-flowered hybrids generally come into bloom too late for us, but there are a few narcissi which are worth mentioning. Narcissus bulbs thrive in rich, well-manured soil protected by slight shade. Waterlogged soil can cause rotting, while drought in late spring retards regrowth, and leads to smaller and possibly fewer flowers the following winter or spring. Plant the bulbs as soon as they are available, in early autumn, or even earlier if possible.

N. asturiensis (syn. *N. minimus*). This miniature Spanish species will reach a height of only 8cm (3in). Tiny yellow trumpets on weak stems appear during mid-winter in most districts. Planting distance: 5–8cm (2–3in).

N. bulbocodium (hoop petticoat daffodil). The wide-open umbrella-shaped golden yellow blooms are carried on stems up to 15cm (6in) high. They appear from mid-winter. This species can be naturalized in unshaded grass, provided the soil is moist. Planting distance: 8–10cm (3–4in).

N. cyclamineus. There are a number of excellent varieties from this dwarf species. Dark green sword-shaped leaves accompany the rich gold drooping flowers with petals that sweep up and back, on stems 15–20cm (6–8in) high. Planting distance: 8cm (3in). 'February Gold' has yellow petals with a deeper golden trumpet, 25cm (10in) high, mid- to late winter; 'February Silver', petals of milky white with a deep yellow trumpet,

25cm (10in) high, mid- to late winter; 'Peeping Tom', all-over yellow, 37cm (14in) high, late winter; and 'Tête-à-Tête', all-over yellow, 20cm (8in) high, two or more flowers per stem, mid-winter.

SCILLA (WILD HYACINTH, SQUILL)

This group of hardy bulbs thrives in warm, sunny borders, in a rock garden or naturalized in grass or woodland. Any type of soil will do, but preferably one containing plenty of humus. The following two species, as a rule, open their flowers in mid-winter.

S. bifolia 'Praecox'. Rich violet-blue star-shaped flowers are carried on contrasting coppery stems. Height: 15–10cm (6–8in). Planting distance: 8cm (3in).

S. tubergeniana. This species looks particularly good when planted among white snowdrops and yellow winter aconites. Star-shaped pale blue flowers, with a central line of turquoise on each petal, are produced in abundance. Height and planting distance: 8–10cm (3–4in).

PART 3
PLANTING & GENERAL AFTERCARE

CHAPTER ELEVEN

THE ART OF PLANTING

The book, till now, has discussed the merits, and some demerits of trees, shrubs, perennials and bulbs for autumn and winter colour. Over 200 types of ornamental plant have been examined for their uses in gardens on many different types of soil. We must now concentrate on the purely practical aspects of growing such plants so that our gardens materialize into the places of beauty we envisage. In many ways this book is topsyturvy, as this part, on the planting and general aftercare of garden plants should be read before you begin creating your autumn and winter features, not afterwards.

Preparation and follow-up attention are so important to all plants. Fail to do this, then at best the results can only be second-rate and at worst they can be so discouraging as to kill all interest and enthusiasm.

I am assuming in what follows that you are not going to pack your bags and move home just because your garden may not have the right conditions for your favourite autumn or winter subject. If this is your problem, take heart. There are very often ways around it and it is usually worth taking pot luck and growing your choice of plant anyway.

There are a few districts where it is impossible to create an attractive garden. A locality will have its limitations, but the range of plants is so wide that practically any situation can be adequately catered for. Even so, there are factors involved which make certain areas less attractive than others, and these must be taken into consideration.

Take clean air, for example. It is a reasonable assumption that no one would live in a smoke polluted district if it were avoidable. Certainly no keen gardener would do so.

Clean air is as important to plants as it is to humans. Then there is the problem of very exposed gardens, making the establishment of new plants a rather exacting and lengthy process. By planting hedging windbreaks, or erecting suitable fencing or walling, it is possible to reduce the wind effect to a large extent.

What about frost pockets? These are depressions or low areas into which cold air drains from the surrounding higher land, so that frost occurs earlier, and lasts longer, than it does elsewhere. Frost pockets should, therefore, be avoided, particularly where winter flowers and autumn berries (which often follow on from spring flowers) are concerned.

The last, and most important, problem faced by aspiring gardeners is that of the soil condition, and this demands careful attention.

SOIL CARE

The most expensive trees and shrubs you can buy will only grow as well as the soil allows. Very few of us have the ideal soil, but it is almost always possible to improve it, regardless of what the problem is.

There are three basic soil types, and each has its own particular characteristics. These are loam, sandy and clay soils. The latter is defined as one in which 30% of the mineral particles measure 0.002 mm or less in diameter. Such soils typically have an extremely sticky texture, which makes them heavy to work. They are generally slow-draining in winter, and bake to a concrete-like carpet in summer.

Sandy soils have 35% of the mineral

The marble-sized berries of *Pernettya mucronata* (prickly heath)
which first appear in autumn, and last until the end of winter.

particles at between 0.10 mm and 0.50 mm in diameter. Unlike clay soils, these are low in essential plant nutrients, which have been largely leached away by rapid drainage over the years. Of course, the good things about sandy soils are that they are very easy to work, and often warm up early in spring.

The final soil type is that of loam, in which clay, sand and silt are present in equal quantities. Consequently, from a gardening point of view, loam soils are the best: they are fertile, free-draining and relatively easy to cultivate, making gardening a real pleasure.

Clay soils

How can problem soils be cured? Let us look at each in turn. The traditional way of handling clay soil is to dig the ground in autumn or early winter, leaving it in large clods (Fig.1). These gradually break down during the winter as a result of the frost. As the soil dries out in spring it should be worked down to a reasonable tilth – the term for a fine, crumbly surface to the soil, making it easy to work and perfect for sowing seeds and planting. Unfortunately this improvement is only temporary, and the soil soon becomes consolidated again.

More permanent improvement can be achieved by digging in heavy dressings of bulky organic matter such as farmyard manure, garden compost, peat or composted bark. The immediate benefit is that the soil is physically opened up. A secondary bonus is that the organic matter is gradually broken down by soil organisms and bacteria into humus, which binds the minuscule clay particles into large clumps. As a result it is easier to work and drains more freely.

Over recent years a great many proprietary soil conditioners have been marketed. Dressings of lime or gypsum cause clumping of clay particles, so these make acceptable conditioners on this type of soil. Concentrated products applied at low rates are unlikely to be successful, because of the sheer bulk of the soil that has to be treated.

Sandy soils

It is, perhaps somewhat surprising to learn that the best way to improve a sandy soil is again to dig in heavy dressings of bulky

Fig. 1 Heavy clay soils should be dug in autumn and left rough, so they can be further broken down by autumn frosts.

Helleborus corsicus produces cup-shaped yellow-green flowers
in late winter.

organic matter. The immediate benefit is that the retenion of both water and plant food is increased. These soils are, quite rightly, described as 'hungry' due, in part, to the leaching of nutrients.

It is not always realized that in sandy soils added organic matter breaks down very quickly, which is why heavy annual dressings are necessary to maintain fertility. These dressings can be either dug into the soil, or they can be applied as a surface mulch. Such mulches reduce water evaporation from the soil, and are gradually incorporated into the soil by the action of worms and insects.

Some sandy soils are acidic, and so benefit from the application of some lime. It is, however, important to check the level of acidity first by having your soil tested. You can have your soil analysed by a laboratory, but it can be expensive. It will be accurate, however, and you will probably be told how to correct any deficiencies. Alternatively you can buy a modern and relatively inexpensive soil-testing kit. Checking the pH level (acidity or lime content) is the easiest and most accurate of the tests you can do at home. The kits vary from 'test-tube' kits in which you add an indicator solution to a sample of soil and compare the resultant liquid against a colour chart, to indicator papers that change colour according to the acidity or alkalinity of the soil. This kind of test is extremely useful when you want to plant a fussy shrub, like a rhododendron, which generally turns yellow and wilts at the slightest hint of lime.

Chalky soils

Chalky soils are usually very shallow, so deep digging should be avoided. They tend to go sticky after a rainfall and, like sandy soils, dry out very quickly. By far the best way of improving these soils is to work in heavy dressings of well-rotted garden compost or manure, and the use of surface mulches.

Another aspect of soil care which should be considered before our chosen plants are sited in their final quarters is that of weed control. Whatever quality your soil is, it is fundamentally important that it is free of harmful perennial weeds such as couch grass, ground elder, bindweed and horsetail. Annual weeds like groundsel, chickweed and speedwell matter much less because they are relatively easily destroyed. It would be pure folly to plant a bed or border which already contains a covering of perennial weeds.

To eradicate these large, established perennials, digging them out rather than hoeing is to be preferred (Fig.2); complete root removal is necessary, otherwise little bits may start to regrow. If time does not permit thorough digging, then chemical control is the next best answer. Weedkillers for perennials must always be used with extreme care. Glyphosate is the most recently

Fig. 2 Before planting it is essential to remove the roots of perennial weeds, such as bindweed and couch grass.

introduced sort, and is applied to the weed leaves mainly in dilution as a spray. It works within a week or two, and the ground treated with it can be planted as soon as the weeds are dead. Most perennial weeds are killed by one application; a few need a second.

The less invasive annual weeds can be controlled similarly by chemical treatment, but a safer and cheaper way is to undertake regular hoeing, which will generally kill the plant at one pass.

PLANTING TREES

We have already discussed the reasons why trees might be included in your garden schemes. They provide height and 'bulk', and whether or not to plant them is arguably the most important decision a gardener can make.

Probably the first point to remember is that deciduous trees (and shrubs) are best planted between mid-autumn and late winter, while evergreens are best moved during early autumn or early spring. Since many subjects are planted during cold months it is, perhaps, necessary to mention that no planting should be undertaken in very wet ground. The soil should be sufficiently moist, so that when you squeeze it in your hand it clings together but falls apart when you let it drop to the ground. In wet areas it is often better to set the plants out after a slight frost. The surface layer of frozen soil can be skimmed off, and the soil beneath may be in a good state for planting.

But what happens if mail-order trees (and this applies to shrubs and perennials, too) arrive when the ground is completely frozen? The answer is simple: heel them in in sand or peat till later, even if it means waiting for a few weeks until winter gives way.

When you purchase your tree it will probably be a slender sapling, about 1.8 m (6 ft) high, and with a spread of 60 cm (2 ft) or more. It is not easy to imagine this as the focal point of your garden, but you should do your best to visualize. Eventually, your sapling may be 18 m (50 ft) high, with a very wide canopy, and even though you will have to wait many years before this happens, you must envisage this final result before you plant. Once a tree is established it is either difficult, expensive or impossible to move it successfully, so it is worthwhile giving much thought to siting and position, before the tree is actually planted. Not all trees reach these kind of proportions, of course, but even the smallest of trees can obscure light if planted too near to the house.

Once you have decided which tree to plant, and where you are going to place it, there are several important planting operations. A hole must be excavated which will contain the roots of the tree when fully expanded. It must be deep enough to bury all the parts of the tree which were buried before, and the soil a good 15 cm (6 in) below this must be dug thoroughly – to allow air into what may be compacted soil, and to allow the free passage of water. These days garden centres offer a wide range of container-grown trees and shrubs. With these it is best to make the hole somewhat wider than the soil ball, as the new roots will tend to spread out sideways rather than downwards.

Until the tree is well established and has made sufficient fresh roots, it will require staking, and the stake should be put into position before the tree is planted. This avoids the possibility of damaging the roots after they are hidden by soil as you drive the stake down. The stake should be at least 1.8 m (6 ft) long, and it should ideally be treated with a timber preservative to give it a longer life. But be careful here. Most wood preservatives, particularly creosote, when freshly applied will damage young plant growth, so unless it was applied to the stake a matter of months before, do not apply it at all.

Supporting a newly planted tree is important. The top of the stake should be positioned so that it is just below the lowest branch of the tree. If it is higher, some of the lower branches could be damaged by it as the tree rocks backwards and forwards in windy weather.

Ties are as important as the stakes. If they grip the tree stem too tightly they will restrict the flow of sap and interrupt growth. If they are too loose they will let the tree rock, and there may be chafing of the stem.

If the tree has any dead, diseased or dam-

Fig. 3 One of the most important aspects of tree planting is the firming of the backfilled soil once the roots are in position.

aged roots, these should be removed before planting takes place. Make every cut as cleanly as possible. Jagged cuts or tears result in rotting, whereas clean cuts can lead to the formation of new, fibrous roots. Of course, with container-grown trees and shrubs, the roots will be relatively undamaged.

It is always a good idea to incorporate some goodness into the soil; peat, manure, well-rotted compost, or one of the number of specially formulated planting mixtures will do. This will enable the roots to penetrate the soil more easily. Once the tree and the stake are in position, backfill the soil (Fig.3). As you do so, remember that the soil will settle over the forthcoming weeks. It is usual, therefore, to tread it down after planting but, even so, the level should be a few centimetres above the surrounding soil. It will soon level out. With trees selected from the open ground (rather than container-grown specimens), where there is bound to have been some root and shoot damage, it is advisable to prune all side-shoots by about a quarter of their length.

PLANTING SHRUBS AND CLIMBERS

Shrubs are different from trees in that they generally sprout branches from ground level, whereas trees have central trunks from which branches radiate. The technique of planting both is the same, except shrubs rarely require the support of a stake in their formative years.

When they are first acquired, shrubs, like trees, are comparatively small and can be expected to grow considerably in height and spread. Many inexperienced gardeners are tempted to grow too many shrubs in one area, with the promise that when they become too crowded, half of them can be taken out. This is completely wrong. In the first place digging up well-grown shrubs requires a great deal of energy, and in the second place the shrubs that you have decided to keep will have distorted shapes; having been crowded

A batch of mixed crocuses: good for planting in a border, or
naturalizing in a lawn.

together for so long, the only way they could grow was up! So, the golden rule with shrubs is to plant a few, with good distances between them, so that there is room for them to spread out naturally. If, for this reason, the bed or border appears sparse, then consider planting a few temporary fillers such as perennials or bulbs.

Climbers and wall plants can give an added dimension to any garden, large or small. When preparing the ground for climbers remember that it is hoped that they will be in position for many years, so preparations should be thorough. To start with, dig the ground deeply; against brick walls you may encounter foundations and as planting in shallow soil is a waste of effort, your only real alternative is to plant a little way from the wall's base. Work in plenty of bulky organic matter as you dig, and a handful of bonemeal or hoof and horn fertilizer around the hole will help to get the plant established.

PLANTING PERENNIALS

The majority of perennials, or hardy border plants, prefer an open situation – open that is to sun, light and air – and by making a careful selection you can achieve variety in form with practically no staking and the minimum of labour generally. As gardeners we are more likely to have a border full of perennials, rather than devoted entirely to shrubs.

Having chosen your site (perhaps you are attempting to overhaul an existing but unsatisfactory border), the first task is to ensure that all perennial weeds are dead. In an old bed, some previously acceptable hardy border plants may themselves have become weedy, and, having retained any worth keeping, it is a good idea to dig out and dispose of the others.

Apply bulky organic matter if the soil is poor, and dig this in thoroughly. It's not a bad idea to add some sharp sand if the soil is clay, (on such a soil it is best to plant during spring,

after the winter frosts have broken down the clods).

As with shrubs, spacing is important but for a different reason. At planting time, in mid-autumn or early spring, the individual plants are probably only a matter of centimetres across, but at their peak of growing they may be a metre across, and perhaps two high. Add to this the fact that our desire is to see the summer border crammed full with stems and leaves, and you can see how important spacing is.

How do we achieve the optimum display from our chosen plants? Many gardeners prefer growing varieties and types in groups – so often the effect is spoiled by dotting plants here and there indiscriminately, even to the extent of duplication. Assuming, therefore, that groups of three or more plants are used of one kind, rather more space should be allowed around each group than between each plant within the group. The average planting space between plants is 40-45cm (16–18in), but between groups it should perhaps be 10cm (4in) more. The tallest growing species naturally require wider spacing, but with the dwarfer or slower growing types it can be less.

PLANTING BULBS

If you purchase bulbs of flowering size and treat them properly, blooms the first flowering season after planting are virtually guaranteed. But how do you recognize a good bulb? This will be heavy for its size, firm to the touch, plump and free from deep-seated blemishes. The largest bulbs available to you are usually the best bloomers, as the flower size is generally in direct proportion to the bulb size.

Bulbs do well in any reasonable soil – in sun or in partial shade – but free-draining soils with plenty of organic matter will naturally produce superior flowers.

Autumn-flowering bulbs should be

A mass of gold only 10cm (4in) from the ground: *Eranthis hyemalis* (winter aconite).

planted from mid- to late summer although, for example, varieties of colchicum often bloom if only placed on a dry saucer indoors – food for the plant was stored the previous season within the bulb.

The winter-flowering bulbs can be planted from early to mid-autumn, although forms of galanthus (snowdrop) are often sold 'in the green' (just after flowering, and before the leaves wither). This is because the bulbs tend to dehydrate if left out of the ground too long.

If you cannot plant your chosen bulbs immediately after purchase, open the bags for ventilation and keep the bulbs cool and dry until you can conveniently plant them.

The technique for planting bulbs depends on where, and for what reason, they are to be grown. Many are planted individually in beds, borders or rockeries. Care should be taken to make sure that the base of the bulb rests firmly on the bottom of the hole. In most cases a trowel will be found the most convenient tool for planting in prepared soil. A dibber, if used, should be blunt-ended, such as an unsharpened sawn-off fork or spade handle.

Many other bulbs look their best when naturalized in lawns, rough grass or wild gardens, where the grass can be left uncut until the bulb foliage dies down. Cheap mixtures of all types of bulbs suitable for naturalizing are frequently offered for sale late in the season and are a good way of planting such sites even if they do not bloom the first year. Informality is the golden rule, and it is an excellent idea to throw out the bulbs in drifts in the selected areas, planting them where they fall.

For this you can use a special bulb-planting tool, which takes out a core of soil from the

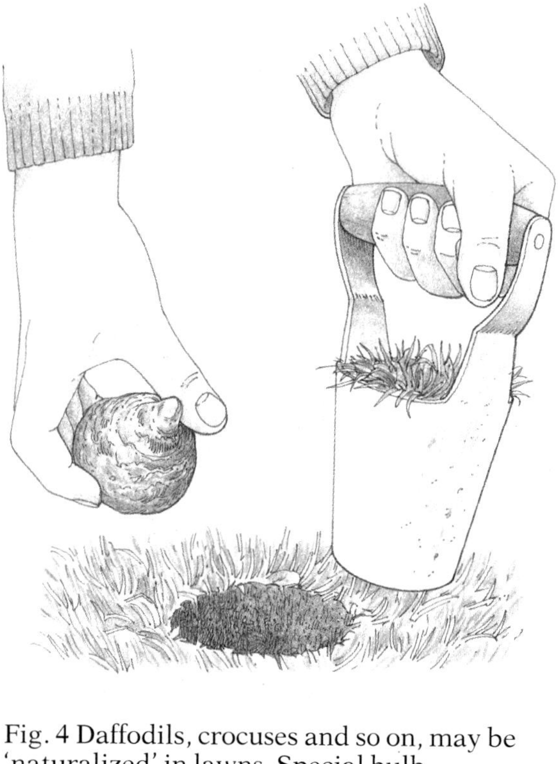

Fig. 4 Daffodils, crocuses and so on, may be 'naturalized' in lawns. Special bulb-planting tools may be used for this.

Table 1. Planting depths for bulbs

Bulb species	Planting depth
Acidanthera	10–13cm (4–5in)
Amaryllis	15cm (6in)
Anemones	8cm (3in)
Chionodoxa	6cm (2½in)
Colchicums	13cm (5in)
Crocosmia	5–8cm (2–3in)
Crocus	5–8cm (2–3in)
Cyclamen	5cm (2in)
Eranthis	5cm (2in)
Galanthus	8cm (3in)
Ipheion	2.5–5cm (1–2in)
Iris (not *I. unguicularis*)	8–10cm (3–4in)
Leucojum	8–10cm (3–4in)
Narcissus	5–8cm (2–3in)
Nerine	10cm (4in)
Scilla	6cm (2½in)
Sternbergia	10cm (4in)

turf (Fig.4). Alternatively, an ordinary spade can be employed to remove a piece of grass with soil. This is replaced when the bulbs have been firmly set in the soil underneath. Once planted, naturalized bulbs can remain undisturbed for a number years, but should be lifted and replanted if they become too thick, or if worn out patches develop.

There is much misleading information given regarding the 'ideal' depths at which certain bulbs are set. While the depth is mildly important, there are even more important things with which to concern ourselves. There are two schools of thought regarding the depth of planting. The first is that the bulbs should be planted at about twice their own depth, and as uniformly as possible. The second is that the larger, taller growing subjects (*Amaryllis belladonna, Colchicum autumnale, Nerine bowdenii*, and so on) should be planted between 10–20cm (4–8in) deep, while minor bulbs (crocuses, snowdrops, *Cyclamen coum*, and so on) can exist at a depth of only 5–10cm (2–4in). There are elements of truth in both theories.

To avoid leaving you on a note of ambiguity, Table 1 lists the appropriate planting depths for the bulbs mentioned in this book. Realize, however, that although I have grown them at these depths, your particular type of soil and locality may cause variations in the degree of success.

CHAPTER TWELVE

GENERAL AFTERCARE

The art of good gardening is directly concerned with the planting and aftercare of plants. Hence, after trees, shrubs, perennials and bulbs have been planted we, as gardeners, must not leave them to their own devices. A whole host of problems will beset our plants if left to Nature. The following sections, if put into practice, will help your chosen plants to become strong and healthy and so avoid many of these natural problems.

FEEDING AND FERTILIZERS

Just as Man cannot live on air alone, neither can plants. There are three main plant foods, and each has its own crucial part to play. The first is nitrogen, which encourages leafy growth and so is good for those grown for their evergreen or decorative foliage (including, of course, the lawn). The second important food supply is the phosphates, which produce strong root growth, so helping new plants to settle in quickly. Finally, potash aids the production of flowers and helps produce good fruits, which speaks for itself where autumn berries are concerned.

Although the above is technically correct, it is only a rough guide, and for normal garden purposes a balanced fertilizer, such as Growmore (which contains all three of the main nutrients) is all that is needed in tree, shrub and flower borders. It is possible to buy fertilizer specially formulated for crops such as roses and chrysanthemums, but it is more sensible to buy an all-purpose type where it is intended for general garden use.

The three main elements so far discussed have to be replenished in the soil relatively frequently, but some soils are deficient in one or more of the 'trace' elements. These are minerals which plants need in minute quantities, just as humans require vitamins. They are usually available in normal garden soils. Fertilizers containing the trace elements should not be applied as a matter of routine, but a few of them may be required from time to time, particularly magnesium. A deficiency of this will show itself in the form of yellowish, mottled leaves with green veins. It is often a problem on sandy soils, but can soon be put right by applying Epsom salts (magnesium sulphate) at 35g per square metre (1oz per square yard).

In many cases the correct application is as important as the correct choice of fertilizer. A few fertilizers, such as bonemeal and some lawn feeds, can be applied in autumn, but the majority should be applied during the growing season. If it does not rain for a day or two after application, it is always worth watering it in. Where granules or powdered feeds are being used it is important not to get it on the leaves, otherwise it might scorch them.

Much fertilizer can be wasted by spreading it carelessly. The weeds may appreciate it, but it will not do the plants much good if you spread it around on mainly bare soil rather than around the root area of the desirable plants. Immediately after application it is a good idea to hoe it in lightly so that it gets to the roots more quickly. General fertilizers, like the granular Growmore, are easy to apply. Usually, an acceptable rate of application would be 60–120g per square metre (2–4oz per square yard), which is one or two handfuls, depending on the current state of your soil fertility.

Do not overlook the liquid and foliar feeds,

mainly formulated for flowers and lawns. It is certainly more troublesome to keep mixing watering cans of fertilizer regularly, but the results can often be speedy and spectacular. These are particularly useful for giving plants a quick boost in summer. Many foliar feeds contain trace elements, too. The whole job is made easier if you use a feed that can be applied through one of the modern hose-end dilutors, designed to be applied in conjunction with watering.

Feeding is a little different where bulbs are concerned. Start to feed at the first appearance of flower stems, the time when a plant needs the most food. From then until the foliage begins to show signs of yellowing and dying down, food can be given once or twice a month. It must be applied direct to the compost, not splashed all over the plant, unless you decide to use a foliar feed. These, however, are not really recommended for bulbs, as the liquid soon falls away from the often sword-like leaves.

LIME AND LIMING

The ideal garden would have a neutral soil, that is, neither too acid nor too alkaline. Here one could grow the widest possible range of plants, and if one type of plant required more lime content, this could be applied artificially; likewise if a plant needs a more acid soil.

If your soil is too acid, it can be rectified by adding lime. This is usually done in winter or early spring after digging. Simply leave it on the surface of the soil, or hoe it in. Do not apply it at the same time as other fertilizers or bulky organic matter. There are three types of lime: ground limestone and chalk (the fineness of grinding is important otherwise it will not be very effective), burnt lime or quick lime (formed when limestone is burnt in a kiln; usually available in large lumps which if placed on the soil absorb moisture and fall to powder), and hydrated or slaked lime (burnt lime which has been slaked down with added water; fine, easy to handle and popular with gardeners). The amount to apply should be determined by soil analysis. When applying any form of lime it is advisable to wear gloves, and keep it away from eyes and mouth.

If, on the other hand, you have a truly alkaline soil, and would like to grow lime-hating plants, use as much peat as you can afford, and use acidic fertilizers such as sulphate of ammonia, flowers of sulphur or aluminium sulphate (but obviously not more than the plants need). The latter type, incidentally, tends to be expensive and is poisonous. Remember, a very limy soil cannot be made more acid in the long term, but the above treatments do have acceptable short-term effects. The acidity or lime content of your soil can have an effect on plant growth as great as any of the major plant foods.

MULCHING

Very hot and very dry weather are generally unsuitable conditions for the healthy growth of plant roots, specially those near the surface of the dust-dry soil. Relief, of course, can be given by frequent watering, but a better long-term insurance against the effects of drought is to mulch the plants; that is, to spread a layer of material over the surface of the soil which will prevent rapid evaporation of the soil moisture. As a result, both the surface and deeper tap roots will be kept cool and moist. As the main object of the mulch is to conserve soil moisture, the ground must obviously be damp when it is applied. If it is dry, it should be watered thoroughly first.

Mulching is a dual-purpose operation. It will also prevent most weed growth, which makes it particularly useful around surface-rooting plants where hoeing cannot be done safely.

Which is the best material to use as a mulch? Ideally, it should be of a spongy

Winter wouldn't be winter without a few drooping heads of
Galanthus nivalis (the common snowdrop).

nature so that it retains moisture, yet at the same time allows plenty of air to pass through so that the roots can breathe. Well-rotted animal manure or compost, straw, peat or leaf-mould are suitable materials. A layer of at least 5cm (2in) thick is necessary for it to be really effective, but this will last for the whole season.

An important point to remember is that a mulch, in covering the soil, also keeps it cool, as it prevents the sun's heat getting through. So, the mulch should not really be applied too early, before the soil has had a chance to warm up slightly. On the other hand, mulching needs to be done before the really dry weather sets in. Late spring and early summer is the best time for application.

When laying down the mulch, specially if it is a strong substance like manure or compost (peat and straw are weak), make sure the material does not rest against the stem of the tree or shrub. Prolonged touching in this way may cause burning and scorching of the outer layers of the stem.

Modern commercial growers, as well as home vegetable and fruit gardeners, use thick black or transparent polythene as a mulching material. This does the job adequately, but tends to be expensive. Another disadvantage is that it does not allow water to pass through, although strips up to 60cm (2ft) wide should let rainwater reach the plants' roots from the sides of the polythene. Modern methods include the use of perforated plastic. However, a carpet of polythene in your flower or shrub border is hardly aesthetically pleasing!

WATERING AND IRRIGATION

If water is not applied early enough, or in sufficient quantity, we are very often disappointed with the growth of our plants. Warmth, food and moisture are the three essentials to plant life. The warmth we get from the sun, and food is supplied naturally and artificially. Too often, though, we do not apply water until our plants are showing signs of drought, by flagging, and by this stage the check to growth may be serious.

If we could only see the amount of water used by gardens, it would be easier to visualize how much soil moisture is lost to the atmosphere through evaporation. Spring is the crucial time for rainfall. At this time of year a garden will use 2.5cm (1in) of water – 24 litres per square metre (4½ gallons per square yard) – every 10 days or so on average.

The golden rule is always to water your plants *before* they begin to suffer, and to keep on watering as and when necessary. Start to think about irrigation as early as mid-spring. If little or no rain falls for 10 days at this time it would probably pay to put on about 7 litres per square metre (1½ gallons per square yard). From late spring onwards twice this amount would be recommended, and three times as much in the height of summer.

These days, if you are prepared to invest, as and when you can afford it, in some modern watering equipment, the job is made much easier. Any good garden shop should be able to offer you a good range of sprinklers, hoses and fittings. Not so long ago a consumer advisory group reckoned that good hoses were not worth the money, but my experience is quite different. After my old hose split and burst a number of times I bought a comparatively expensive braided hose, and after 10 years out of doors it is still in excellent condition, and promises to give perhaps another 10 years of good service. While on the subject of hoses, for ease of storage you can't beat a 'flat' hose that is wound into a cassette. For an average garden a hose will suffice, but if you have an acre or more you should consider burying the hose and using 'pop-up' water points around the garden.

As, in this book, we are mainly concerned with tree, shrub and flower borders, most of the oscillating or travelling sprinklers are too large for our purposes. However, there are small sprinklers covering a circle of, say, up to 6m (20ft) in diameter, and these labour- and time-saving watering accessories should be considered.

Finally, while household tap water is suitable, rainwater is best for plants. This can be collected from roofs and gutters by rigging up a small network of drain pipes and a water butt. If you must use tap water, remember that really hard water should not be used for rhododendrons and other lime-hating plants.

WEEDING

There are weeds, and there are weeds, if you know what I mean. I draw the distinction between weeds that, to be frank, are little more than a nuisance around the flower and vegetable garden (these include groundsel, chickweed and annual grasses), and the weeds that are major problems and compete extremely effectively with the plants that we are endeavouring to cultivate. The distinction is not strictly between annual and perennial types (as discussed on p.103), but it is between those that are easily controlled, by chemical or hoe, and those that quite definitely are not. We have already looked at weed control as an aspect of soil preparation before we plant. The only point I would add, while discussing the aftercare of plants is that we must, wherever possible, maintain a programme of constant weed control. If allowed to develop they will take moisture and nutrients from the soil, as well as competing for light in the upper regions. In addition, many weeds harbour, and make excellent breeding grounds for, insect pests and diseases.

PRUNING

If we were to undertake a survey to determine which of the many jobs in the garden was considered to be the most complicated and confusing, I am sure that pruning would come at the top. To start with there is the problem of knowing when to prune, then deciding what to cut out, or does your plant need pruning at all? Generally, a judicious bit of snipping will bring you a better display of bloom, crop of fruit and cover of foliage, as well as making your plant healthier. Plants very often outgrow the space allocated to them, and in many instances pruning will cut them down to size, so that they don't crowd out other subjects. Then again, some trees and shrubs become unsightly when vigorous, awkwardly placed shoots upset the balance. Pruning is the answer here, too.

Before we look at the pruning of trees and shrubs in their own rights, we should be clear on the correct tools to use and techniques to employ. Where tools are concerned there are three basic types: saws (where a serrated single blade is moved to and fro to eat through the stem); cutters (secateurs, loppers and shears which have a scissor-like action with two blades) and knives (single blades that are 'pulled' through the stem to sever it).

Pruning saws have wide-set teeth to lessen the risk of jamming, through clogging with the soft, moist sawdust. Saws should not be used as a matter of routine, however. Use them only for removing branches that secateurs or loppers cannot cut, perhaps anything over 2.5cm (1in) in diameter. Electric or petrol-driven chain saws are recommended for branches, stems or trunks over 15cm (6in) in diameter, but these are expensive items of equipment, so it is more common for gardeners to hire them by the day or weekend. Safety is an important factor with all pruning tools, but particularly with chain saws, as flying chippings can be a problem – wear goggles or some other form of eye protection.

Secateurs are probably the most important pruning tool. There are two main types: the anvil, with a soft-metal plate which supports the stem while the single hard-metal blade cuts through it, and the parrot-beak or by-pass types which cut like a pair of scissors, though only one of the blades has a cutting edge.

Loppers and pruners are modified versions of the by-pass secateur with handles perhaps 45 cm (18 in) long. These are useful for cutting out old, hard wood which is too thick and tough for ordinary secateurs. If you do not enjoy ladders and heights, you would be wise to invest in a tree lopper – a by-pass secateur attached to the end of a pole perhaps 3.6 m (12 ft) long. These are invaluable for cutting out high branches which would otherwise be out of reach.

Clipping hedges is very much an act of pruning, and a pair of hand shears is by far and away the best tool to use. The mechanical trimmers tend to tear stems and rip leaves but, it has to be said, are ideal for large gardens where there are long and wide hedges. Using an electric or petrol-powered trimmer will save many hours of hard and strenuous labour.

Knives are not used widely these days as their use requires a degree of expertise, so they are mainly left to professionals who know exactly how much pressure to put on the blade, and in which direction to point it. If you prefer to use a knife, however, make sure it is sharp. Hold the branch that is to be cut below the point where the knife comes into contact. With the knife behind the branch make the cut by drawing the knife upwards, at an angle.

But where on the stem should we make our cuts? Any shoot on which leaves or flowers are borne should be examined closely, to determine where the buds lie; a pruned stem must always terminate with a bud. And the cut must be as reasonably close to the bud as possible without damaging it, perhaps 0.5–1 cm (¼–⅓ in) above the bud. If a cut is made between two buds, but the tip of the pruned shoot is a long distance from the bud below it,

there is nothing to draw the sap up the shoot, so it will gradually die back. We are then left with a 'snag' – a dead piece of wood resulting from incorrect pruning.

Trees

Trees will normally develop according to their natural habit, but they often need a little guidance if they are going to give an optimum display. Take, for example, a standard tree with 1.5–1.8 m (5–6 ft) of clear trunk. In the nursery before they are sold, these should be encouraged to form a strong unbroken stem with a vigorous leading shoot and moderately short side branches. To maintain the tree as a standard, the careful cutting out of some of these side growths must be carried out regularly as the trunk lengthens. Also, remove any 'casual' shoots which have the audacity to appear on the cleared trunk.

'Feathered' trees have branches coming from the trunk, almost down to ground level. Some gardeners prefer to see a tree clothed to the base with branches and leaves, but this has certain disadvantages if grown on the lawn. Light and moisture will be prevented from getting to the grass, and it will probably be difficult to use the lawnmower satisfactorily.

From time to time gardeners who possess fully grown, established trees, will need to remove complete branches. If the branch is long and too thick to be cut easily with secateurs, it should be sawn off in manageable stages.

Branches of any width should be undercut first, by perhaps as much as a third of their diameter (Fig. 5). Then cut from above, slightly further out from the trunk than the undercut. The remaining bit of branch should fall cleanly. Fail to reduce the branch in this way and you run the risk of the weight bringing the branch down, and possibly tearing a strip of bark down the side of the tree (Fig. 6).

When you get to the stage of having a stub about 30–45 cm (12–18 in) long, a final cut from above should remove it cleanly. It is a good idea to pare the wound (with a sharp knife) to a smooth surface. It will then be more sightly, and make a better surface for the application of an all-important wound sealant. Sealants are used to protect and seal heartwood, so that insect pests, fungal diseases and virus infections do not gain entry.

Shrubs

Unlike garden trees, shrubs generally require regular and careful pruning if they are to provide us with an attractive, long-lasting display. In general, pruning should be done in winter (or just as growth starts in spring), when the shrubs are least likely to suffer a shock to their systems. If major surgery is required it would be as well to spread it over two or more years; although some do not object to a single huge operation, others will not take too kindly towards it.

The deciduous autumn-flowering shrubs which bear their blooms on the current season's stems are pruned each year, around mid-spring, just as growth is starting. This is done in order to give the flowering wood the optimum period of time in which to develop and ripen. The previous year's growth should be cut back hard to within one or two buds of where it joins the older wood.

On the other hand, deciduous winter-flowering shrubs carry their flowers on stems produced during the previous growing year. These should be pruned as soon as possible after the blooms have faded. The operation comprises the complete removal of all the one-year-old stems from which the flowers arose. This encourages young shoots to grow, and these will become the flowering stems the next year.

Then, of course, there are the evergreen shrubs. These should really be left unpruned, unless you want to cut back their size or alter their shape. They generally start to make new growth much later in the spring, and it may well be the height of summer before growth

becomes really vigorous. This is the best time to prune as the full effect of the past winter can be assessed, and any damaged growth removed at the same time.

Earlier in the book, when we looked at winter shrubs, we discussed species of cornus

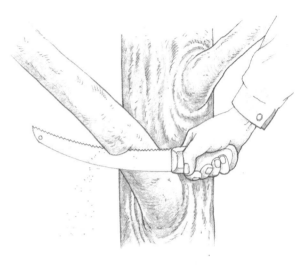

Fig. 5 Before large, heavy tree branches are pruned, they should be undercut a little way from the trunk.

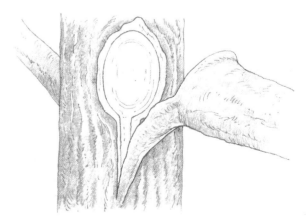

Fig. 6 Failure to undercut an unwanted branch sufficiently may result in the bark tearing down the side of the tree.

and salix, which produce highly decorative stems during our coldest months. These should be cut back severely, to a bud within 30cm (12in) of the ground in spring, to encourage new, vigorous growth.

Other shrubs, like the rhododendron, dislike regular pruning, and just do not demand it. With these, however, dead-heading should be practised (Fig. 7). This – also an act of pruning – is essential if you are to maintain quality and quantity of flower. If the old, faded blooms are allowed to stay on the plants and form seed, few flower buds are likely to be produced the following year. The removal of the large flower heads can be done quickly by hand; trusses can be snapped off between finger and thumb.

Roses, some of which have worthwhile autumn flowers, also require dead-heading (Fig. 8). With some types this can be combined with reducing the height of the flowering stems during autumn. With a pair of sharp secateurs, cut off 23–30cm (9–12in) of the fading flower head. This helps prevent the plant being rocked about by autumn gales.

There are, however, a number of instances where shrubs, which are normally pruned after the flowers have faded, should be left alone. These include the roses grown for their large, decorative autumn hips, and the many shrubs chosen for their berries and fruits. Where these are concerned, it is up to the individual gardener to decide whether he wants colour in autumn at the expense of future seasonal flowers, or better spring/summer blooms with no autumn berries.

PERENNIAL PLEASURE

Hardy border plants are not pruned, at least, not in the way shrubs are. Most border

Fig. 7 At the end of the rhododendron flowering season, the old heads should be snapped off by hand.

Fig. 8 Faded rose blooms should be 'dead-headed', using a pair of sharp secateurs.

perennials need attention in late autumn, after their season of glory. A number of plants (including *Anemone japonica*, phlox, Michaelmas daisies, and so on), produce woody stems which die down after their autumn displays. These will then need cutting back, mostly down to ground level, to make way for fresh growth the following spring.

This is the ideal time, when the border is conveniently bare of topgrowth, to do a whole range of necessary cultivations. For a start, do any hoeing to get rid of annual weeds, or dig out the deeper-rooted perennial kinds. Bindweed, which may have taken hold during summer, should be carefully dug out at this time. Do not throw any of its stems or roots on the compost heap; they may take root and grow.

I have always been keen to lay a good bulky mulch of manure or compost on the perennial border. I do this in mid-spring, in readiness for the forthcoming growing season, but some gardeners do the job in autumn. It will, naturally, keep the soil slightly warmer, so does afford a degree or two of winter protection.

Many of our autumn- and winter-flowering beauties do not have to undergo regular annual shearing off at ground level. Bergenias, hellebores, primulas, violas, pulmonarias and several others produce only soft, green fleshy stems, not the woody type that dies back each autumn.

After three or four years of continuous growth, your border plants may have reached a stage where they are too big for their space, or are not performing as well as they once used to. This is when we can undertake division of the plants. Herbaceous plants should really only be divided in spring or autumn. Choose a mild day when the soil is moist, but not wet. Dig up the clump with a fork, taking care not to damage the roots more than necessary. Shake off the excess soil and study where the basic divisions should

be. The smaller plants, such as primulas and pulmonaries, may be broken up by hand, taking off pieces bearing both shoots and roots. But if the clump is too large or tough for this, then use two hand or garden forks. Push these into the centre of the clump and prise apart gently (Fig. 9). A sharp knife may be used to sever any tough roots. Another method of dividing a plant, although rather more haphazard, is to chop the clump apart with a spade.

Fig. 9 Some border perennials can be propagated by division in spring, using two garden forks back-to-back.

Before the main daffodil season in spring, there are a few winter-flowering miniatures. Here we have *Narcissus cyclamineus* 'Peeping Tom'.

Keep only the divisions which come from the outer region of the clump – dispose of the central older part of the plant. Replant the divisions as soon as possible, and make sure they are watered in thoroughly.

As already mentioned on p.51, border phlox tend to suffer from eelworm, which lives in stems and shoots. With this group of plants, therefore, do not divide them – instead take root cuttings during winter.

OUTDOOR BULBS

Usually, bulbs in beds or borders in the garden will have to be lifted after flowering to make way for other temporary bedding plants, but if this is not necessary, then narcissi, in particular, are best left undisturbed for three or four years. After this period of time the expanding colonies of bulbs can become overgrown, resulting in poorer flowers. During the bulb's dormant period (when the foliage has withered away completely), dig up the clumps carefully, divide the bulbs – with your fingers – and replant the largest ones in new sites. Move the smaller 'baby' bulbs (known as offsets, bulblets or cormlets) to an out-of-the-way spot. These may take a season or two before they are large enough to produce flowers. At planting time it is advisable to add a handful or two of bonemeal to the square metre (yard) around the hole. This will help the plants to become established.

When lifting mature bulbs for storing until the next year, they should not be laid out to dry in the sun (as we ripen, for example, onion crops), as this will dry them out too quickly and may also render them liable to attack by the small narcissus fly. Trays with netting or open slatted bottoms are most suited for ripening and storing, which should take place under cover in an open, airy shed.

On p.95 we looked at the winter-flowering *Iris unguicularis* (Algerian iris). This is a plant with rhizomatous, not bulbous roots. These are underground 'runners' which act both as roots and a means of propagation. Most of us are familiar with the way strawberry plants are increased; they throw out above-ground runners, which eventually root and get a hold on the soil to form a new plant. This iris (and many other summer-flowering species) acts similarly, but with underground runners. When it is time to lift and divide an overgrown clump of this iris, carefully dig around the clump of rhizomes and raise them gently so that the roots are retained. Shake off the excess soil and with a sharp knife divide up each rhizome into sections, so that each piece bears leaves or buds above and roots below. Discard all old and diseased pieces, and then replant each retained section at the same depth as the original plant. Unlike other rhizome irises, because it is a winter bloomer, this species should be divided in early autumn.

PESTS AND DISEASES

Unlike fruit and vegetables, trees, shrubs and flowers are not grown in large groups of one particular type, and this has the effect of making outbreaks of pests and diseases less serious. There is certainly no need to spray them all as a matter of routine. However, troubles do occur from time, to time. Some, such as rose black spot, are confined to a particular group of plants, while others like greenflies and vine weevils do not discriminate. Where concentrations of one type of plant do occur, preventive measures should be adopted rather than last-ditch attempts at wiping out severe infestations.

There are several general problems which are likely to attack any number of the plants mentioned in this book. Among these troubles are greenfly and blackfly. These are easily killed by spraying (Fig. 10) with a specific aphicide (which will not harm beneficial insects like ladybirds and bees). However, the chemical will not always kill the freshly laid eggs. These will hatch and mature normally (adults are created in less than two weeks). Consequently, repeat applications should be made at intervals, as recommended on the containers.

Then there is honey or bootlace fungus, which is present in most woodlands and can be deadly to some shrubs and yet leave others unaffected. Rhododendrons and magnolias can suffer badly, but camellias scarcely ever appear to be affected. The plants attacked wilt, turn brown and die back for no immediately apparent reason. Parts of hedges may go brown and die; small creamy-coloured toadstools may appear at the foot of the plant, and black bootlace-like strands may be found in the soil. The answer is to destroy any badly infected plants (sad though

Fig. 10 Aphids can be controlled on a host of garden plants by regular spraying with systemic insecticide.

this may be). Alternatively, use the proprietary Armillatox or Jeyes Fluid, following the manufacturer's recommendations. It is a particularly difficult disease to cure.

Ants can be a nuisance in gardens, and even indoors when infestations are bad. They 'milk' greenfly on cultivated plants, in much the same way that we milk cows. There are a number of very potent gel and powder destroyers on the market, which are very effective.

Slugs devour the young leaves and shoots of many hardy border plants. They can be killed by poisoned bait placed under a propped up tile or slate (in an attempt to keep them away from cats, dogs and birds) next to the susceptible plants. The slug pellets need to be replenished when they become wet and soggy. Much cheaper, but not always so effective, is to use slug traps. Sink an old yoghurt carton into the soil, its rim level with the surface, and fill it with beer. In the morning empty out the slugs and snails which will have crawled in and drowned overnight.

Roses, popular though they are, probably have more problems as a plant group than any other. Capsid bugs are green insects which puncture and distort young leaves. The leaf edges then turn brown and look sickly. A systemic greenfly killer will usually cure the problem. Caterpillars eat the leaves of roses (and a host of other trees and shrubs). In isolated cases hand pick the culprits off and destroy them; spray larger infestations with a recognized caterpillar killer. This will very often control the troublesome caterpillar of the leaf-rolling sawfly, too. This is an insect which causes the leaves to be rolled up longitudinally. Cuckoo spit appears as blobs of white froth at stem tips. Inside each mass of bubbles lurks a tiny sap-sucking insect. Rub the blobs off by hand in small outbreaks, but control larger infestations by spraying forcefully with fenitrothion.

Where rose diseases are concerned, black spot is the most easily identified. Blackish purple spots 5 mm (¼ in) in diameter appear, on the lower leaves first, then later higher up the plant. They eventually join together, and the leaf turns yellow and falls prematurely. This is a disease which should be prevented (rather than cured). Spray with a suitable fungicide at fortnightly intervals from mid-spring. If the disease gets a hold, help to control its spread by picking off infected leaves and destroying them, or by burning all fallen leaves at the end of the season.

The other common fungal disease of roses is mildew. Leaves, stems and thorns are covered with white powder, and the plants are severely weakened. Again, picking off and destroying the leaves is recommended, along with fortnightly sprays from mid-spring of a suitable fungicide. As always, prevention is better than cure, and if you grow open-stemmed disease-resistant varieties, the problem is greatly reduced.

Rhododendrons are not without their problems. The fungus disease known as 'bud blast' causes considerable damage to flower buds of evergreen species and hybrids. The first symptoms appear between mid-autumn and early winter, when infected buds turn grey or brown. The fungus is not apparent until spring when it develops on diseased buds as tiny black bristly structures, each bearing a pin-head of fungus spores from which the disease spreads. The fungus is thought to be transmitted by leafhopper insects which lay their eggs in the buds. Attempt to control the insects, and you invariably reduce the bud blast infestation. Spray the plants with fenitrothion insecticide two or three times during late summer.

Vine weevils are universally troublesome. Their larvae damage the roots of many greenhouse pot plants, while the adults cause havoc outdoors, eating the leaves of rhododendrons and other ornamentals (as well as strawberries and raspberries). They are usually night-time feeders, hiding during the day under the soil or in plant debris. Control

can be effected, not least by good garden hygiene – clear away unnecessary plant debris and use sterilized compost in the greenhouse or potting shed. Where the pest occurs, a persistent insecticide, such as gamma-HCH, applied as a dust or spray to the foliage, soil or potting composts, gives good control.

Michaelmas daisies, colourful though they are in autumn, are prone to a particularly nasty 'wilt'. The trouble is caused by a microscopic fungus that lives in the roots. It emits a toxic poison which passes through the sap, killing the leaves. There is no cure once the plants have been infected. Prevent future problems by burning diseased plants, and propagating only from those known to be healthy. Do not replant in the same position as the disease is soil-borne.

These autumn border flowers, however, suffer with another insect problem: the eelworm. This will also damage a number of other ornamental plants, including some asters. The pests penetrate leaf and stem tissues, turning the leaves dark brown in areas between the veins, gradually spreading across the whole leaf. Severe infestations check growth and kill plants. There is, unfortunately, no sure chemical treatment, but dormant crowns or 'stools' can, during winter, be plunged into hot water 45°C (115°F) for five minutes. Otherwise dig up and burn any infested plants.

Dahlias, on the other hand, are prone to attack from the familiar earwig. To a lesser extent chrysanthemums and clematis are also attacked by this pest. Both young and adult insects make ragged holes in the blooms and leaves, usually during the night. Removal of garden debris reduces the available resting sites, and gamma-HCH sprayed on and around the plants will eliminate the insects. You may prefer, however, to trap the insects in inverted flower pots filled with straw. To kill the sheltering earwigs, empty the pots every day into a bucket of boiling water.

As we have discovered, holly trees (species of ilex) can be grown either for the variegated foliage or colourful fruits – or both. Only one real problem occurs with holly: that of the leaf miner. The maggots of this small fly tunnel into the leaves causing unsightly irregular galleries across the leaves. The trees generally suffer little, but growth of young specimens may be checked, and some leaves may drop. Minor infestations can be picked off by hand, or if necessary, spray regularly with gamma-HCH during spring and summer.

Outdoor bulbs are generally trouble-free. Narcissi and daffodils tend to be the most troubled, but the problems are not too serious, and can be controlled relatively easily. When naturalized types produce leaves but no flowers, there are two likely causes: blindness or narcissus fly. The former is caused mainly by the bulbs being too small. The answer is to plant only large, plump bulbs, and to keep the soil moist at all times. When narcissus fly is present, no flowers are produced, the leaves are grassy and lack vigour. A large caterpillar will be found in the bulb if cut open. To avoid this pest buy your bulbs from a reputable supplier who has treated them. When the naturalized clump has been diagnosed as being infested by the fly, dust the leaves and soil every two weeks after flowering until early summer with gamma-HCH. Destroy any infested bulbs in store. Similarly, stem and bulb eelworm can be prevented by buying only healthy, treated bulbs, and by destroying any that are found to be infested. Symptoms of the presence of this pest are distorted leaves, mottled with yellow, with distorted (or absent) blooms. Also, when sliced open, the bulb has brown rings inside.

The final message must be to grow your plants well. If they have plenty of food, light and moisture, they are far better equipped to shrug off pest and disease attacks than weak, hungry and thirsty plants. When you are baffled by a plant pest or disease, don't be afraid to ask for advice. Local gardening societies, allotment holders, the Royal Horticultural Society (if you are a 'fellow') or the national gardening magazines will usually be willing to help you out.

APPENDIX:
LIST OF USEFUL ADDRESSES

It would be impossible, here, to list every supplier of trees, shrubs, border perennials and bulbs. However, the following is a selection of some highly reputable suppliers, who each have extensive lists of available plants or bulbs.

Trees and shrubs
Chris Bowers & Sons, Whispering Trees Nurseries, Wimbotsham, Norfolk, PE34 8QB.
Everton Nurseries Ltd., Everton, Nr. Lymington, Hants., SO4 0S2.
Highfield Nurseries, Whitminster, Glos., GL2 7PL.
Hilliers Nurseries Ltd., Ampfield House, Ampfield, Romsey, Hants., SO5 9PA.
Reginald Kaye Ltd., Waithman Nurseries, Silverdale, Carnforth, Lancs., LA5 0TY.
Knap Hill Nurseries, Barrs Lane, Knaphill, Woking, Surrey, GU21 2JW.
Notcutts Nurseries Ltd., Woodbridge, Suffolk, IP12 4AF.
Scotts Nurseries (Merriott) Ltd., Crewkerne, Somerset, TA16 5PL.
Sealand Nurseries Ltd., Sealand, Chester, CH1 6BA.

Roses
Anderson's Rose Nurseries, Cults, Aberdeen, Scotland, AB1 9QT.
David Austin Roses, Bowling Green Lane, Albrighton, Wolverhampton, WV7 3HB.
Peter Beales Roses, London Road, Attleborough, Norfolk, NR17 1AY.
Fryer's Roses, Knutsford, Cheshire, WA16 0SX.
Gregory's Roses, Stapleford, Notts., NG9 7JA.
Harkness Roses, The Rose Gardens, Hitchin, Herts., SG4 0JT.
LeGrice Roses, Norwich Road, North Walsham, Norfolk, NR28 0DR.
John Mattock Ltd., Nuneham Courtenay, Oxford, OX9 9PY.

Border perennials
Bressingham Gardens, Diss, Norfolk, IP22 2AB.
Beth Chatto, White Barn House, Elmstead Market, Colchester, Essex, CO7 7DB.
Holden Clough Nursery, Holden, Bolton-by-Bowland, Clitheroe, Lancs., BB7 4PF.
Hopleys Plants Ltd., High Street, Much Hadham, Herts., SG10 6BU.
Kelways Nurseries, Langport, Somerset, TA10 9SL.
J. & E. Parker-Jervis, Marten's Hall Farm, Longworth, Abingdon, Oxon., OX13 5EP.
R. V. Roger Ltd., The Nurseries, Pickering, North Yorks., YO18 7HG.

Bulbs
Walter Blom & Son Ltd., Coombelands Nurseries, Leavesden, Watford, Herts., WD2 7BH.
Rupert Bowlby, Gatton, Reigate, Surrey, RH2 0TA.
Broadleigh Gardens, Barr House, Bishops Hull, Taunton, Somerset, TA4 1AE.
De Jager, The Nurseries, Marden, Kent, TN12 9BP.
Lowland Nurseries, Spalding, Lincs., PE12 6DZ.
Peter Nyssen Ltd., Railway Road, Urmston, Manchester, M31 1XW.
J. Parker, 452 Chester Road, Old Trafford, Manchester, M16 9HL.
Van Tubergen, Oldfield Lane, Wisbech, Cambs., PE13 2RJ.

INDEX

Abelia × *grandiflora*, 32
Abeliophyllum distichum, 71
Acer capillipes, 65
 davidii, 65
 griseum, 65
 grosseri hersii, 65
 japonicum, 12
 palmatum, 12
  p. 'Dissectum', 32
  p. 'D.Atropurpureum', 32
  p. 'Senkaki', 65
 pennsylvanicum, 65
 platanoides, 12
Acidenthera bicolor murielae,
 55–57, 108
Aconite, winter, 92
Aconitum carmichaelii, 48
Aesculus hippocastanum, 11
Air pollution, 98
Alder, 65
 common, 66
 grey, 66
Alnus, 65
 glutinosa, 66
 incana, 66
Amaryllis belladonna, 57, 108, 109
Amelanchier canadensis, 12
Anemone hepatica see *Hepatica*
Ants, 121
Arbor-vitae, 69–70
Arbutus × *andranchnoides*, 66
 unedo, 66
Ash, common, 62
Aster amellus, 50
 × *frikartii*, 50
 novi-belgii, 50
 pests, 122
 Stoke's, 54
Autumn colour, 9–60
Azalea, 32
 Ghent, 32
 Knap Hill, 32–34
 mollis, 34
Azara microphylla, 66

Barberry, 34
Bark colour in winter, 62
Berberis × 'Buccaneer', 34

 thunbergii, 34
Bergenia 'Abendglut', 84
 'Ballawley Hybrid', 84
 crassifolia, 84
Betula costata, 66
 nigra, 66–68
 papyrifolia, 68
 pendula, 68
Birch, 66
 paper, 68
 red, 66
 river, 66
 silver, 68
Bird nuisance, 10
Bittersweet, climbing, 71-72
Black spot, 121–2
Blackfly, 120
Blackthorn, 26
Bladder cherry, 32
Border plants for autumn colour,
 47–54
 for winter colour, 84–89
Boston ivy, 42
Box, Christmas, 71, 83
 sweet, 83
Bramble, 82
 whitewashed, 71, 82
Bud blast, 122
Bugbane, 50–51
Bulbs, aftercare of, 120
 for autumn colour, 55–60
 for winter colour, 90-96
 pests, 123
 planting, 106–9
Bush clover, 41–42

Callicarpa bodinieri giraldii,
 10, 34
Camellia, 30
 sasanqua 'Narumi-gata', 34
Capsid bugs, 121
Carpinus betula, 11
Caryopteris × *clandonensis*, 34–36
Castor oil plant, 75
Caterpillars, 121
Ceanothus 'Autumnal Blue', 37
 × 'Gloire de Versailles', 10,
 36

Cedar, blue Atlas, 68
 Western red, 70
 white, 70
Cedrus atlantica 'Glauca', 68
Celastrus, 71–72
 orbiculatus, 72
Centranthus ruber 'Coccineus', 50
Cercidiphyllum japonicum, 12–14
Chaenomeles speciosa, 36
Chalky soils, 102
Cherry, Japanese, 24–26
Chestnut, horse, 11
Chilean firebush, 30
Chimonanthes praecox, 64, 71, 72
Chinese lantern, 52
Chionodoxa, 108
 gigantea, 91
 luciliae, 91
Chrysanthemum, 48
Cimicifuga foetida, 50, 51
Clay soils, 100
Clerodendron trichotomum
 fargesii, 36
Climbers, for autumn colour, 30–
 46
 for winter colour, 71–83
 planting, 104–6
Cobnut, 14
Colchicum, 108
 autumnale, 57, 109
 luteum, 91
 speciosum, 55, 57
Coneflower, 52
 purple, 51
Cornel, 14
Cornus, 117
 alba, 72
 florida, 14
 kousa chinensis, 36
 nuttallii, 14
 stolonifera, 72
  'Flaviramea', 71, 72
Cortaderia selloana 'Sunningdale
 Silver', 51
Corylus avellana, 14
 C. a. 'Contorta', 68
Cotinus coggygria, 36
Cotoneaster, 14

conspicuus 'Decorus', 38
'Cornubia', 14
horizontalis, 72
'Hybridus Pendulus', 14
lacteus, 38
Cowslip, 86
Jerusalem, 88
Crab, flowering, 23–24
Crataegus, 14
monogyna, 14–16
prunifolia, 16
Crimson flag, 54
Crocosmia × *crocosmiflora*, 57–58, 108
Crocus, 108
autumn, 55, 57
chrysanthus, 91–92
imperati, 92
saffron, 58
sativus, 58
speciosus, 58
tomasinianus, 92
Cyclamen, 10, 108
coum, 92, 109
hederifolium, 55, 58
Cydonia speciosa see Chaenomeles
Cypress, swamp, 29

Dahlia, 47–48
pests, 123
Daphne mezereum, 64, 71, 74
odora, 74
Dead-heading, 117
Diseases, 120–3
Division, 118
Dogwood, 14, 72
yellow, 71

Earwigs, 123
Echinacea purpura, 51
Eel-worm, 122
Elaeagnus × *ebbingei*, 74
pungens, 71
Elephant's ears, 84
Elm, English, 11
Embothrium coccineum, 30
Eranthis, 108
hyamelis, 92
× *tubergenii*, 92
Erica, 74
carnea, 74–75
× *darleyensis*, 75
mediterranea, 75
Eucryphia glutinosa, 16
× *nymansensis* 'Nymansay', 16
Euonymus alatus, 38

europaeus, 38
fortunei, 75
japonicus, 75

Fatsia japonica, 75
Feeding and fertilizers, 110–11
Filbert, 14
Firethorn, 42
Flowers for autumn colour, 10
for winter colour, 62
Flower-of-the-incas, 94
Fothergilla major, 38
monticola, 38
Fraxinus excelsior, 62
Frost pockets, 98
Fruit for autumn colour, 9–10
for winter colour, 64
Fungus disease, 121

Galanthus, 108
elwesii, 94
nivalis, 94
n.reginae-olgae, 94
Garrya elliptica, 75–77
Gleditsia triacanthos 'Sunburst', 20
Glory-of-the-snow, 90
Golden honey locust, 20
Goldenrain tree, 20
Gorse, 30
Grass, pampas, 51
Greenfly, 120
Gum, red, 23
sweet, 20–23

Hamamelis × *intermedia*, 38–41, 77
japonica, 41, 77
mollis, 41
Hawthorn, common, 14–16
Hazel, 14, 62
corkscrew, 68
Heath, 74–75
prickly, 80
Heather, 74–75
Hebe, 41
× *andersonii* 'Variegata', 41
'Autumn Glory', 41
Hedera, 77
canariensis, 78
colchica, 78
helix, 78
Helleborus, 84–86
atrorubens, 86
corsicus, 86
foetidus, 86
niger, 86

orientalis, 86
viridis, 86
Hepatica nobilis, 86
Hippophae rhamnoides, 41
Holly, 20
pests, 122
Honeysuckle, 78
winter, 71, 78
Hornbeam, 11
Hyacinth, wild, 96
Hypericum 'Hidcote', 41
× *inodorum*
'Elstead', 41

Ilex × *altaclarensis* 'Golden King', 20
aquifolium 'Bacciflava', 20
a. 'J. C Van Tol' 20
Ipheion uniflorum, 94, 108
Iris, 94, 108
danfordiae, 94–95
histrioides 'Major', 95
reticulata, 95
unguicularis, 95, 120
Ivy, 77
Boston, 42
Canary Island, 78
common, 78
Persian, 78

Japonica, 36
Jasmine, winter, 78
Jasminum nudiflorum, 78
Juneberry, 12
Juniperus communis, 11

Koelreuteria paniculata, 20

Laurustinus, 83
Leaf for autumn colour, 9, 30
for winter colour, 64
Leaf miner, 122
Lespedeza thunbergii, 41–42
Leucojum vernum, 95, 108
Leycesteria formosa, 4
Lilac, Californian, 36
Lily belladonna, 57
kaffir, 54
Lime, common, 11
Lime and liming, 111
Liquidamber styraciflua, 20–23
Liriodendron tulipifera, 23
Liriope muscari, 51
Loam soils, 100
Lonicera fragrantissima, 71, 78
standishii, 78
Lungwort, 88

Macleaya cordata, 47
Magnolia campbellii, 68
  disease, 12
  grandiflora, 10, 23
Mahonia bealii, 78
  'Charity', 78
  japonica, 78
Malus, 23–24
  'Golden Hornet', 24
  'John Downie', 10
  tschonoskii, 24
Maple, 12, 32, 65
  coral bark, 65
  Father David's, 65
  paper bark, 65
  snakebark, 65
May, 14–16
Metasequoia glyptostroboides, 24
Mezereon, 64, 71, 74
Michaelmas daisy, 10, 50, 122
Mildew, 122
Monkshood, 48
Montbretia, 57–58
Mountain ash, 26–29
Mulching, 111–12

Narcissus, 95, 108
  asturiensis, 96
  cyclamineus, 96
  fly, 123
Nerine bowdenii, 58, 108, 109
Nyssa sylvatica, 24

Oak, 24
  common, 11
  red, 26
  scarlet, 26
Obedient plant, 52
Oxlip, 86

Pachysandra terminalis, 80
Pampas grass, 51
Pansy, garden, 88–89
Parrotia persica, 24
Parthenocissus henryana, 42
  quinquefolia, 42
    tricuspidata 'Veitchii', 42
Peach, Chinese, 69
Perennials, aftercare of, 117–20
  for autumn colour, 47–54
  for winter colour, 84–89
  planting 10
Pernettya mucronata, 80
Persian ironwood, 24
Pests, 120–3
Pheasant berry, 42
Phlox paniculata, 51–52

Physalis alkekengii franchetii, 52
Physostegia virginiana 'Vivid', 52
Pincushion flower, 52
Pine, Scots, 11
Pinus sylvestris, 11
Poplar, Lombardy, 11
Poppy, plume, 47
Populus, 68
  × *canescens*, 69
  nigra 'Italica', 11
Primrose, common, 88
Primula, 86–88
  allionii, 86–88
  edworthii, 88
  elatior, 86
  juliae, 88
  veris, 86
  vulgaris, 88
  'Wanda', 88
Pruning, 114–17
Prunus, 24–26
  davidiana, 69
  'Fudanzakura', 69
  'Kanzan', 24
  sargentii, 26
  serrula, 69
  spinosa, 26
  subhirtella 'Autumnalis', 69
Pulmonaria officinalis, 88
  saccharata, 88
Pyracantha atalantioides, 42
  coccinea, 42
  rogersiana, 42–44

Quercus, 26
  coccinea, 26
  robur, 26
  rubra, 26
Quickthorn, 14–16
Quince, flowering, 36

Redwood, dawn, 24
Rhododendron, 30, 80–82, 117
  auriculatum, 80
  arboreum, 82
  'Christmas Cheer', 82
  disease, 121, 122
  mucronulatum, 80, 82
  'Praecox', 82

Rhus typhina, 26
Rosa, 44, 117
  moyesii, 44
  pests and diseases, 121–2

  rubrifolia, 44
  rugosa, 44
Rose, Christmas, 86
  guelder, 46
  Lenten, 86
Rowan, 26–29
Rubus biflorus, 82
  cockburnianus, 71, 82
Rudbeckia fulgida, 52
  'Goldsturm', 52

St John's wort, 41
Salix, 117
  alba 'Chermesina', 71
  babylonica, 11
  daphnoides, 69
  matsudana 'Tortuosa', 69
Sandy soils, 98–100, 102
Sarcococca, 82
  confusa, 71, 83
  hookerana digyna, 83
  humilis, 83
Saxifraga fortunei, 52
Scabiosa caucasia, 52
Schizostylis coccinea, 54
Scilla, 108
  bifolia 'Praecox', 96
  tubergeniana, 96
Sea buckthorn, 41
Sedum spectabile, 54
Shadbush, 12
Shrubs for autumn colour, 30–46
  for winter colour, 71–83
  planting, 104–6
  pruning, 116–17
Skimmia japonica, 44
Slaking, 103–4
Sloe, 26
Slugs, 121
Smoke tree, 36
Snowberry, 46
Snowdrop, 58, 92–94
Snowflake, 95
Snowy mespilus, 12
Soils, chalky, 102
  clay, 100
  loam, 100
  sandy, 98–100, 102
Sorbus, 26–29
  aria, 26
  aucupuaria, 26–29
  'Embly', 29
  hupehensis, 29
  'Joseph Rock', 29
Spindle tree, 38
Spirea, blue, 34–36

Spotted dog, 88
Spurge, Japanese, 80
Squill, 96
Starflower, spring, 94
Sternbergia lutea, 55, 60, 108
Stewartia pseudocamellia, 29
Stokesia laevis, 54
Stonecrop, 54
Stranvaesia davidiana, 44
Strawberry tree, 66
Sumach, stag's horn, 26
Sycamore, 11
Symphoricarpos albus, 46
   × *doorenbosii*, 46
Tassel bush, 75–77
Taxodium distichum, 29
Taxus baccata, 11
Thorn, 14–16
Thuja, 69–70
   occidentalis 'Rheingold', 70
   plicata, 70

Tilia × *europaea*, 11
Trees for autumn colour, 11–29
   for winter colour, 65–70
   planting, 103
   pruning, 115–16
Tulip tree, 23
   pink, 68
Tupelo, 24

Ulex europaeus, 30
Ulmus procera, 11

Valerian, 50
Veronica, shrubby, 41
Viburnum betulifolium, 46
   davidii, 46
   opulus, 46
Vine weevil, 122
Viola odorata, 54
   × *wittrockiana*, 88–89
Violet, sweet, 47, 54

Virginia creeper, 42
   Chinese, 42
Vitis coignetiae, 46
   vinifera 'Brandt', 46

Watering and irrigation, 112–14
Weed control, 102–3, 114
Whitebeam, 26
Willow, scarlet, 71
   violet, 69
   weeping, 11
Wilt, 122
Windbreaks, 98
Windflower, 57
Winter colour, 62–96
Winter sweet, 64, 71, 72
Witch hazel, 38, 77
   Chinese, 41, 77
   Japanese, 41, 77

Yellow star flower, 55, 60
Yew, common, 11